"*Kingdom First* is a deeply personal yet universally resonant exploration of what it means to truly seek first the kingdom of God in an unraveling world. With rich storytelling, practical wisdom, and spiritual insight, Bob bridges the gap between ancient truths and modern struggles. This book is not merely a reflection on faith—it is a call to action, urging believers to live authentically, build transformative communities, and embody the hope of Christ in everyday life."
—ALAN HIRSCH, founder, Movement Leaders Collective

"In *Kingdom First*, a wise sage offers up priceless lessons on being Christians in these post-Christendom times. Drawing on years of ministry experience, with stories across several different cultures, Bob Roxburgh reminds us of some simple practices of being Christ's church in the culture. After years of fatigue, grasping for the straws of church success, *Kingdom First* comes to us as a gift. Read it slowly and allow yourself the time to be renewed in a vision for the church for these disruptive times."
—DAVID FITCH, Lindner Chair of Theology, Northern Seminary, Chicago

"This is a book rich in wisdom, insight, and experience. The combination of knowledge and the delightful recounting of stories makes an enjoyable and memorable read. The last chapter on leadership is particularly helpful and readers may well wish to read this chapter a number of times. Bob's wide experience of different cultures and contexts helps him to convey the lessons of a lifetime."
—MARTIN ROBINSON, national moderator emeritus, Fellowship of Churches of Christ in Great Britain and Ireland

"Bob has been thinking and talking about the church all his life. Like many of us, he believes it should be missional. But missional for Bob means people not programs, stories not strategies, disciples not decisions. I am delighted he has put all of this into a book. As the present incumbent of his beloved Millmead, I heartily recommend *Kingdom First* to you."
—IAN STACKHOUSE, senior pastor, Millmead, Guildford Baptist Church, United Kingdom

"Take a walk down memory lane in the company of an experienced leader whose considered reflections provide not only insights into the man himself but to the values that shaped his life and contributed to him having a remarkable, fruitful ministry. Accompany him and gain wisdom and encouragement from his life's journey."
—ROY SEARLE, cofounder, Northumbrian Community

"Bob shares his warm and wise anecdotes around the frame of living in and for the kingdom of God. He shares thoughtfully and vulnerably from a life lived in service to the King and his people across denominational and international boundaries. His immersion in Scripture and his able application of God's word in this strange post-Christendom location offer food for the journey and encouragement for the road."
—LEN HJALMARSON, author of *No Home Like Place*

KINGDOM FIRST

KINGDOM FIRST

Lessons Learned and Fulfillment Gained
by Seeking God's Kingdom in a Troubled World

Robert L. Roxburgh

Foreword by Stanley Biggs

WIPF & STOCK · Eugene, Oregon

KINGDOM FIRST
Lessons Learned and Fulfillment Gained by Seeking God's Kingdom in a Troubled World

Copyright © 2025 Robert L. Roxburgh. All rights reserved. Except for brief quotations in critical publications or reviews, no part of this book may be reproduced in any manner without prior written permission from the publisher. Write: Permissions, Wipf and Stock Publishers, 199 W. 8th Ave., Suite 3, Eugene, OR 97401.

Wipf & Stock
An Imprint of Wipf and Stock Publishers
199 W. 8th Ave., Suite 3
Eugene, OR 97401

www.wipfandstock.com

PAPERBACK ISBN: 979-8-3852-4109-5
HARDCOVER ISBN: 979-8-3852-4110-1
EBOOK ISBN: 979-8-3852-4111-8

03/26/25

THE HOLY BIBLE, NEW INTERNATIONAL VERSION®, NIV® Copyright © 1973, 1978, 1984, 2011 by Biblica, Inc.® Used by permission. All rights reserved worldwide.

To my wife, Brenda, whose wisdom and devotion
helped us all as a family (Cameron, Graham, Heather)
to seek first the kingdom of God.

Contents

Foreword by Stanley Biggs — ix

Preface — xiii

Acknowledgments — xvii

Introduction — xix

Preview of Topics — xxvii

CHAPTER 1: Entering the Kingdom — 1

CHAPTER 2: Kingdom and the Church — 11

CHAPTER 3: A Tale of Two Cultures — 23

CHAPTER 4: Community and Mission — 38

CHAPTER 5: Worship and Devotion — 55

CHAPTER 6: Leadership and Character — 75

EPILOGUE: Into an Increasingly Troubled World — 98

Discussion and Interaction — 119

Bibliography — 127

Foreword

BEFORE YOU SETTLE IN for a journey with Bob Roxburgh in search of the kingdom, come backstage for a moment and meet my friend.

This indomitable "Scouser" was born in Liverpool, home of the Beatles, where residents are known as such. Recently, Bob returned from what he playfully called his "farewell tour of England." Advent, the highlight of his year, was launched by visiting many friends, including those with whom he had pastored, with other leaders. Even though years have flown by, there has been no diminishment of reciprocal love and respect. One former parishioner exclaimed,

> When you came our way, we were off the rails. By the time you left, we had found our way. And now, years later, we're flourishing.[1]

By his life and ministry, Dr. Robert Roxburgh declares the good news that "the kingdom is very near!"

Perhaps you feel "off the rails" with culture and even the church you have loved, left, and avoided since. Bob's lifelong passion is that you seek and find the kingdom within.

Were this foreword to be a headstone, it could well read, "He Lived Dialogically."

Scholars describe dialogic space as "a platform to look at the situation from more perspectives than one, create room for discussion, and seek mutually beneficial consensus."[2] So, what makes this complicated but straightforward leader tick?

---

1. Conversation with Robert Roxburgh; the speaker's identity is not recalled.
2. Smiech, "Conversations That Matter."

FOREWORD

HE LIVES DIALOGICALLY

Bob listens. He questions with respect and insight. Those who think much differently encounter the same thing as those who don't: humor, wisdom, and compassion, along with an unforgettable cup of hot English breakfast tea (with a side of cream and "I mean HOT").

But there's more, and it counts. He tells the truth. After reading the original manuscript, a friend who meets with us monthly observed, "Bob, your writing is authentic. You didn't hide your failures."[3]

Brokered through passionate humility, Bob has at his command a memorized library of hymns, poetry, and quotes, frequently inserted in conversations at just the right moment.

Famed author and poet John Milton lost his eyesight in midlife, and about his blindness, he wrote words often referenced over coffee or lunch with friends:

> "Doth God exact day-labour, light denied?"
> I fondly ask. But patience, to prevent
> That murmur, soon replies, "God doth not need
> Either man's work or his own gifts; who best
> Bear his mild yoke, they serve him best. His state
> Is Kingly. Thousands at his bidding speed
> And post o'er Land and Ocean without rest:
> They also serve who only stand and wait."[4]

Such is also the lot of those who can almost see the end of the road. As our platforms seem to shrink, influence wanes, and we are tempted to give up and roll over, we are arrested by Milton's anguished question: "Does God exact day-labour, light denied?" Whether you are beginning your own journey, frustrated at midlife, or feel you can almost see the end, he concludes, with Bob, "They also serve who only stand and wait."

With a mysteriously warm twinkle in his eye, Bob invites us for a canopy tour of his life and that of others who sought first the kingdom of God. I can almost hear him humming one of his favorite hymns, "At Even, Ere the Sun Was Set," as we settle in for an adventure!

The last verses . . .

---

3. Paul Martinson, conversation with the author, Dec. 2024.
4. Milton, "Sonnet 19," lines 7–14 (emphasis mine).

Foreword

Thy touch has still its ancient power;
no word from thee can fruitless fall:
Hear, in this solemn evening hour,
and in thy mercy heal us all.[5]

STANLEY BIGGS
Advent
Kelowna, British Columbia

---

5. Twells, "At Even," stanza 7.

Preface

MANY YEARS AGO WHEN I was in my mid fifties, after only eighteen months in leadership at a church full of promise in the American Midwest, I resigned. My wife, Brenda, and I made a sad journey by road back to her parents' home in Oakville, Ontario. Our world had fallen apart, and we were at a loss, not knowing what came next. We entered that unknowing space, where one walks by faith not sight and the future is uncertain. These types of vulnerable, uncertain times are forges for faith and character. We all have stories about events that have shaped our lives; some experiences were joyous, others sad. Even the most cursory reading of the book of Genesis reveals such a wide range of human foibles.

As a follower of Christ, I have lived many years as a husband, father, neighbor, friend, athlete, and motorcyclist. I was also in church leadership for fifty years. I believe others can benefit from my experience, so I hope these reflections can encourage us in these difficult times in which we live. I also want to share what I have learned about the challenges of Jesus' teaching in his call to "seek first his kingdom and his righteousness" in Matt 6:33. I hope to give insight into such issues as spirituality, community, worship, and leadership (in its numerous forms), for any Christian community, whatever its structure.

Each person's reflections or insights are unique and limited to a personal understanding of life, perhaps augmented by education and experience. Particularly at my age, I can look back at the evolution of my life. Things such as my view of self, love, marriage, living as a believer in the world, and my understanding of God, the church, and its leadership, have all evolved. While being guided by my trust in the Bible, much of my thinking had to change as I observed dramatic shifts in the society around me.

Preface

> The illiterate of the 21st century will not be those who cannot read and write, but those who cannot learn, unlearn and relearn.[6]

I am fortunate to have spent almost equal amounts of my life in the United Kingdom (with its closeness to European culture) and Canada, as well as ten years in the United States. I have been educated and have served in churches and organizations in all three countries. Living in different cultures has helped me see a wider world and grasp a bigger picture of life in God's kingdom through the richness of various outlooks.

FOR WHOM I WRITE

I want to write about the importance of Matt 6:33 to those who seek leadership in several levels of life, such as family, local community, small groups, or pastoral leadership in a local church. My desire and bias as an adult has been to experience intergenerational life in both culture and the church so that all people hold an equal place in my heart and mind. For several years I belonged to a breakfast discussion group with mostly guys in their fifties and older, until two young women in their thirties showed up. For about three years, we were together each Tuesday morning. The world opened up for the guys as they got to know the female mind and personage better, and they helped us all understand the new world that had been growing around us. The two women in the group were very sharp and articulate. One of their friends asked them why they would bother attending an "old men's club," to which they replied that they needed the insight and wisdom of those who had experienced life over many years. As for me, I was able to keep in touch with the thinking of generations younger than I because of the presence of the two women at our Tuesday breakfasts. I write with the mindset that I am sharing my story and insights among men and women whom I consider equal in every way.

In chapter 6 I will write about leadership, and I hope to wrestle with the questions and issues that are being faced today: issues like leaders helping their church community to recognize that the world is radically different, and that the pastor is no longer the expert with all the solutions. I will ask questions such as, What kind of leadership is needed now? How do we refocus our leadership work and our church perspectives from individuals to community?

---

6. Toffler, *Future Shock*, 271.

Preface

What I write is not intended for an academic readership per se. There are numerous personal stories and other narratives that start each chapter; they are geared toward underlining important issues about living in our present culture. While each chapter expresses concepts already covered by others at a far deeper level than the reflections presented here, the *notes* section at the end of each chapter offer theological and philosophical support to a number of issues raised therein.

While I write with a good educational background, my primary focus is upon applying practicalities to my experiences as a Christian leader. Once in a conversation with my brother, Alan, we discussed growing up in Liverpool, England, and I mentioned to him that an American university offered a course about the life and philosophy of the Beatles. Alan reminded me that I had lived among them and was raised in the same culture as they. He noted that such an experience was full of rich value, whatever any academic course had to offer about the Beatles; that is part of the tone of this book.

I do not write for those seeking new ideas for the church or how it might be more "successful." Given all that we face in today's culture, I'm not sure that would be helpful. I believe that the time for finding organizational fixes for the church is over. Instead, we need a period of waiting on God, listening to what he is doing, as well as opening our minds and hearts to discern what he is saying to us, particularly in our local neighborhood or parish. It is not an easy task, but my hope is that in *seeking first the kingdom of God and his righteousness*, we will best be able to do that.

FORMAT

I will share stories and reflections that I have experienced on my journey, as well as other narratives that are not particularly personal. I will also present *insights* which grow out of those stories. I will then conclude with *points to ponder* that offer practical help and ideas for further personal reflection or community life. At the end of each chapter, there will be two sections: *appendix* and *notes*. The appendix will contain suggestions for books, articles, or websites to encourage those wanting to pursue topics further. By following this method, I hope to help the reader catch the flow of the narrative. At the end of the book, there will be a section designed to facilitate discussion and interaction. All Scripture references will be in the New International Version (2005) unless otherwise indicated.

Acknowledgments

THERE WILL NOT BE many authors whose book has not received help and input from others; mine certainly has.

My family, including my sons, Cameron and Graham, as well as my brother, Alan, urged me to major in stories, as did various friends, local and abroad.

Stan Biggs spent many hours coaching me to be down-to-earth and personal in what I wrote. He kept me on an important trajectory throughout.

Kelly Madland and Ally Badry of our church community did many important revisions for which I had no skills.

My daughter, Heather, aided by her own offspring, has made a remarkable contribution through her prodigious efforts to get the book into correct format. I am deeply thankful for her crucial work that helped me to persevere.

Introduction

THERE IS A DEEP search among many to find meaning and purpose in life. The theme of the kingship of God, a central motif in Scripture, addresses this search and this longing. In Matt 6:33 Christ's dictum to "seek first his kingdom and his righteousness" is an offer to believers of meaningful life and inner security as they face an unraveling world. Each chapter describes my understanding of what it means to "seek first his kingdom and his righteousness" and how these words of Jesus address our current crises. My desire is that through sharing some of my own journey and its accumulated insights, God's people may be assisted in forming communities shaped by the kingdom. I do not try to cover the waterfront but limit myself to the topics noted in the contents above.

MY INNER STRUGGLE

Advent is a special season for me as I celebrate the Incarnation. I enjoy some of the well-known cultural expressions of Christmas, which I have celebrated at home with my family and in numerous European Christmas markets and festivals. I am aware that there are differences between this season as the secular culture experiences it and my own understanding of the purpose of Advent.[1] Christmas is not just about God coming into the world but about God's kingdom dawning upon humanity, offering a whole new way of life with a new set of priorities and goals. In the birth of Jesus, we not only have the presence of God with us but we have the kingdom of God in person. It is the kingdom of God that provides us with the true meaning of Advent. I realize too that just as secular values have shaped parts of my Christmas, in a similar manner I have been shaped also by this culture's norms and values in my everyday life.

1. John 1:14.

Introduction

All we do and how we live and think as Christians is so contrary and antithetical to the secular world. In Isa 11:1–9 we are given one of the great passages prophesying the coming of the Messiah. In those verses we are shown a different King, one upon whom the Holy Spirit rests and who has wisdom and understanding. He will judge through righteousness. The Messiah/King is different, and he leads a different kingdom, one in which the normal order of things can be turned upside down or go the opposite way of the norm, such as the wolf living with the lamb. (An excellent read on this subject is Donald Kraybill's *The Upside-Down Kingdom*.[2]) We see this clearly when we read the words of Jesus to Pilate in John 18:36; Jesus said, "My kingdom is not of this world. If it were, my servants would fight to prevent my arrest by the Jewish leaders. But now my kingdom is from another place." The world is changing so dramatically that it is harder to know how to live for the kingdom. So many things we relied on are fading. What we once perceived as "normal" will not return.

MATTHEW 6:33

We are instructed to pray for and seek the kingdom before all else. The main part of that *seeking* is a relationship with Christ. We all face pressures around security or the desire to be successful. It is easy to judge ourselves and others around the ways we fall short of this vocation. When Jesus instructs us to "seek first his kingdom and his righteousness" (Matt 6:33), it is in the context of his teaching on the practicalities of life, such as food, shelter, clothing, and the like. He wants to help us understand where our true security and fulfillment lie.[3] Christ is teaching us how this new kingdom works. He draws a comparison between life in the kingdom and the life most live.[4] He shows us there is a new reality available. No longer are we on our own, trying to navigate life in our own strength. Christ is urging us not only to seek the inner reality of the kingdom but also the practical outworking of the kingdom in our daily lives (which he calls righteousness). To seek first his kingdom in every aspect of our pilgrimage is the most fulfilling of all the other options that are before us in a troubled world. It will require that we trust God and choose to live with his perspective. Seeking first his

---

2. Kraybill, *Upside-Down Kingdom*.
3. Matt 6:19–34; Luke 12:22–34.
4. Matt 6:25–32.

INTRODUCTION

kingdom and his righteousness is not a given in the lives of many. I share the struggle to fully grasp its implications in my own life.

THE KINGDOM?

Wheaton College is my alma mater. Its motto is *Christo et Regno Ejus*, which means "For Christ and His Kingdom." The very subject, kingdom of God, has given rise to many scholarly books that seek to define what it is, how it affects (transforms) our lives, and how it can impact the way in which we as God's people live with love and care in the places where God has planted us. The idea of a kingdom seems foreign to our twenty-first-century culture. External authority is seen as intrinsically oppressive, mostly because it has been that way throughout the centuries. It is difficult to share the Christian life with a secular world in terms they understand when ideas like "monarchy" indicate the absence of autonomy or the inclusion of control, all at a time when many forms of institution and governance are being rejected, especially in the light of a postcolonial world.

The kingdom of God is fundamentally God's sovereign rule expressed and realized through the different stages of redemptive history.[5] Jesus talked about the kingdom in several of his parables and that the gospel was about the coming of *God's* kingdom rule through Jesus Christ.[6] Prior to the coronation of a king in Israel, the concept of God as King was about his care for his people as well as his rule.[7] Jesus believed in rule but not in the way of *lording over others*. The essence of the word "king," as the New Testament sees it, is submission to one who can offer us both the most *fulfilling* life and the opportunity to serve him for the most *purposeful* life. Living for the kingdom must be more than the idea of submission to a powerful potentate governing our personal lives.

The emphasis of *Decolonizing Evangelicalism: An 11:59 p.m. Conversation*, by Randy S. Woodley, Bo C. Sanders, and Grace Ji-Sun Kim, is that the church not only proclaims the kingdom of God but must also demonstrate God's kingdom by living out God's will for the communities in which we live.[8] The same emphasis is shared by the Mennonite scholar John Driver

---

5. Mark 1:15.

6. Matt 13:44–46, 52.

7. 1 Sam 8:10–22. What is interesting is that Jesus names himself as "King" in Matt 25:35–40.

8. Woodley et al., *Decolonizing Evangelism*.

Introduction

in *The Kingdom of God: Goal of Messianic Mission*.[9] As with Driver, my conviction is that God's kingdom demonstrates an alternative order to human social organizations.

A dear friend asked me recently what I might perceive to be the difference between kingdom and church. Intellectually, I could try to respond to this by referring my friend to the author Scot McKnight. In his book *Kingdom Conspiracy*, McKnight makes the case for the kingdom and the church being equal parts of one expression.[10] I reaffirm Scot's position and yet realize that so much of the life and work of churches do not always reflect kingdom principles or values. My heart also senses something more is required to answer my friend's question. Rather than the kingdom being an extension of an institution, I sense it to be about what God is up to in the world by the power of the Holy Spirit, into which dynamic the church is invited.[11]

There is a legend supposedly attributed to Martin Luther about the healing of the lame man in Acts 3, telling of the time Luther was being shown around Rome as St. Peter's cathedral was being built. He was shown all the magnificence of the Catholic order in Rome at the time. The story goes that his guide said to him, quoting what Peter had said to the lame man (and I paraphrase), "Martin, we no longer have to say 'Silver and gold have we none.'" To which Luther retorted something like, "Alas, I fear that no longer as a result can we say, 'In the name of Jesus, rise up and walk.'"

Understanding what the kingdom is and how it works is perhaps difficult for many in this age because it is hard for people to line up the kingdom that Jesus taught with the kingdom that most of us want. This is part of the struggle for those who see the church in terms of political power or for those whose view of success orbits around material gain or popularity.

An example of kingdom and church at work happened at Guildford Baptist Church, England, before I was called to be its pastoral leader. It had experienced a long history downtown and was growing rapidly under the preaching of David Pawson; then the town council needed the property on which the church building stood. An agreement was made to provide an adequate alternative property on which to build a new facility. The church

---

9. Driver, *Kingdom of God*.

10. McKnight, *Kingdom Conspiracy*.

11. In Luke 10:1–12 and Matt 10:1–8, the seventy are sent by Jesus to declare that "the kingdom of God has come near to you" and that he would be in their midst with the power to heal, restore, and renew. Acts 2:42–46 is a post-resurrection extension of these passages.

Introduction

felt that a site later to be named Millmead, just across the River Wey, was ideal for them because it was right downtown where thousands went shopping and attended the theater and restaurants daily. That began a long, drawn-out, and tension-filled journey with a leading councillor who was responsible for each phase of the negotiations; he was opposed to selling the Millmead property to the church.

Eventually a date was set for the city council to vote for or against the proposal. The church congregation spent days praying and walking around the property, believing that God wanted them to acquire it in order to build a place that would have an impact on the city. The councillor who opposed the church took ill and couldn't attend the council meeting. The topic was raised on the agenda, and in effect someone expressing that the church had been not well treated for far too long proposed that, for the sum of one pound sterling (about two dollars), the property be sold to the church. Soon after, the church built the Millmead Centre (designed by a leading London architect), which served not only the church congregation but other organizations in town. The effective ministry and size of the congregation grew, as did its reputation both in the city and the UK. Today, many years later, its ministry and facilities have been expanded to include a riverside cafeteria and various cultural events. I know that hundreds of congregations worldwide could tell similar stories. These things are not just the result of human effort and ingenuity, they are the unique and sovereign work of the Holy Spirit among people who are open to his leading.

These stories of Luther in Rome and of Guildford Baptist Church in England give some insight into my friend's question about kingdom and the church. I think he was asking if the Holy Spirit, working in his own way for the kingdom, supersedes the plans and projects of the church in general. My one caution is that we need to keep before us the reality that many of our experiences, whether we call them kingdom or church, happen in the ordinary and everyday events of life, not always in the unusual or dramatic.

Dr. Les Biggs, for many years the lead pastor at Elk Lake Baptist Church in Victoria and then professor at Carey Theological College, University of British Columbia, Vancouver, offers his own answer to my friend's question about church and kingdom. Here is a brief extract from chapter 2 of his treatise *The Challenge of Understanding the Kingdom of God*, a project submitted in partial fulfillment of the requirements for the degree of doctor of ministry in Vancouver, May 2011:

Introduction

For the Kingdom of God is not a matter of talk but of power. (1 Cor. 4:20). Many ministry contexts are devoid of the kind of works associated with the breaking in of the Kingdom, whether it is the miracle of someone entering the Kingdom, or exorcisms, or healings. The power of God will have more impact than any advertising or programmatic element of ministry. Indeed, the coming of the Kingdom is true ministry. The Kingdom of God has become an abstract concept disconnected from the past, disconnected from the dynamics of daily Christian life. For many Christians, the Kingdom of God does not connect them to any recognizable story line in any recognizable way. Connecting the life of the Church to the Kingdom of God will entail an ongoing conversation between our understanding of the Kingdom and our way of being a Church. The local Church, once it understands and incorporates the Kingdom of God into its ethos will realize that its goal is not to run programs to meet the needs of its own but rather to live to participate in the mission of God.[12]

RIGHTEOUSNESS

The word *righteousness* within Matt 6:33 can get overlooked or cause tension that we subconsciously avoid. I am also concerned that we can think of righteousness as a complicated endeavor only to be experienced by the spiritual elite. Righteousness is, in part, about simple, practical, down-to-earth living for ordinary folk wanting to make God's kingdom their vision and way of life. For example, reading through the Sermon on the Mount often will go a long way to helping us live this way.[13]

It is also important to note that righteousness doesn't just come about by gritting our teeth and trying harder. The impetus comes from the Holy Spirit, as these verses reveal so tenderly:

> Our blest Redeemer, ere he breathed
> his tender, last farewell,
> a guide, a Comforter, bequeathed
> with us to dwell.
>
> And every virtue we possess,
> and every conquest won,

---

12. Biggs, *Challenge of Understanding*, 19.
13. Read Bonhoeffer, *Cost of Discipleship*, and Willard, *Divine Conspiracy*.

Introduction

and every thought of holiness,
are his alone.[14]

I am not disposed to comment on all the variables that Christians express about the Holy Spirit, such as a second experience named *baptism* or *fullness*, which some believe is received after conversion. Several stories I tell in this book reveal my conviction that the role and ministry of the Holy Spirit in both our personal and corporate lives is meant to be very significant. I once said at a church conference that much of our theology about the Holy Spirit is influenced by our non-experience of his power in the daily life of the church. In churches and movements where the power of the Holy Spirit is believed and taught, I have observed and experienced both the wonderful impact of their ministries as well as, alas, some abuses and hyperbole. The biblical evidence is that while the dramatic and amazing acts of the Spirit are true, it is also true that God's Spirit works among ordinary folk in the ordinary circumstances of life.[15] There is an emphasis on spiritual gifts in the New Testament, but there is also evidence that the Holy Spirit is within us to produce Christian character.[16]

Experiencing righteousness in our personal devotional life is the ministry of God's Spirit. James Houston in *The Transforming Friendship* writes that the Holy Spirit is the friend who makes heaven real to us.[17] Paul urges us to go on being filled with the Spirit.[18] Prayer, worship, and Scripture meditation are the means that help us keep in step with the Spirit. In our human frailty, that fullness can evaporate so quickly. Jesus tells about a friend knocking at the door at midnight for some bread to illustrate that we need to ask, seek, and knock earnestly, and that the promise of the replenishment of the Spirit's power will be there. It is not a matter of *feeling* but of *faith*.

In the sixth century AD, a Celtic monk named Dallan Forgaill wrote the Irish poem "Rop tú mo Baile" (Be Thou My Vision), and Eleanor Hull versified the text into what is now a well-loved hymn/song among young and old. These two verses express my deep sentiments in what I write about Matt 6:33:

---

14. Auber, "Our Blest Redeemer," verse 1 and 4.
15. Acts 8; Rom 15:17–19.
16. 1 Cor 12; Eph 4; Gal 5:16–25.
17. Houston, *Transforming Friendship*.
18. Eph 5:18–20.

Introduction

Be thou my vision, O Lord of my heart;
Naught be all else to me save that thou art.
Thou my best thought by day and by night;
Waking or sleeping, thy presence my light.

Riches I heed not, nor vain, empty praise;
Thou mine inheritance, now and always.
Thou and thou only, first in my heart,
High King of Heaven, my treasure thou art.[19]

---

19. Hull, "Be Thou My Vision," verse 1 and 4.

Preview of Topics

IF YOU WERE HAVING coffee with me at a local Starbucks and you asked me what I was, in simple language, getting at in my book, here it is.

My underlying emphasis is that by following Matt 6:33 we will find the most encouraging approach to how to live in our present troubled world and, as a result, bear testimony to faith in Jesus Christ. I will try to keep a tone of hope and encouragement through each of the topics. I will affirm so much of what is written by Christian scholars who have shined a light on the struggles of both the church and our individual lives. I don't want to offer new philosophies, theories, or programs, but instead I want to reflect and give insights from my journey. I once had a conversation with a pastor who was struggling with the fact that so many in his congregation seemed to lack understanding of Christian commitment and values. I reflected that one of the reasons might be that they needed a fresh understanding of the nature of the kingdom. The conversation I had with that pastor is one of the ways that this book got its impetus.

CHAPTER 1: ENTERING THE KINGDOM

I will share the importance of a transforming experience of Jesus Christ, however that comes about. I will tell the story of my own conversion that initiated my journey into making God's kingdom and righteousness the goal of my life. I will note also that it is a testimony, not a template. We are a redeemed people seeking first the kingdom of God. We recognize that we belong to a kingdom that will last forever. We have an inheritance secured for us by the cross of Christ.[1]

It is vital for believers to understand that our faith is far more than church attendance, rather it is based on the experience of 1 Pet 1:3–9. This

---

1. Col 1:13–14.

should be constantly before us as a Christian community in all that we seek to do. There are many ways to express our faith. We need the filling of God's Spirit to be motivated to do so. We need also to expand our view of the kingdom. Of course, it is about our desire to serve the King, but it is also about our comprehensive understanding that the kingdom involves the reign of Christ in all aspects of personal and social life.

CHAPTER 2: KINGDOM AND THE CHURCH

I will express Christ's love and commitment to the church as the basis of my own love and commitment to it. Being part of some form of Christian community is an important way of *seeking first the kingdom*. God is still at work, and it is his view that the church, as part of the kingdom, will prevail, but we need fresh understanding of how that needs to happen. The church has been marginalized by the culture and pushed from the front seat to the back seat. To understand the disappearing influence of Christians in the West, one must realize that the church is no longer at the center of things and that the culture has devalued it. Instead of trying to recapture the past or return the church to a place of status, the church must learn to function on the margins. The need to listen to God in the light of Scripture is paramount. We must keep our eyes and hearts open to what God is saying to the church while at the same time living out Matt 6:33 in our individual and corporate lives. I list some of the many writers, churches, and organizations that can offer help to leaders discouraged by wanting to serve God in such a difficult and disruptive time.

CHAPTER 3: A TALE OF TWO CULTURES

Christ's own words give us the clearest mandate: "They are not of the world any more than I am of the world. My prayer is not that you take them out of the world but that you protect them from the evil one" (John 17:14–15). We are a part of life around us, and we are to live in our context as Daniel and his friends did in theirs. What they offered was a willingness to serve the Babylonian culture well while at the same time being resolved to stand up to it, as the fiery furnace in Dan 3 and the lions' den in Dan 6 clearly reveal. My stories herein are meant to reveal the opportunities that exist to be involved deeply with and show love for those in the culture in which we live without compromising Christian values. Dallas Willard in his book *The*

Preview of Topics

Allure of Gentleness expresses that we must be transformed people living out a life reflective of Jesus himself—a life of love, humility, and gentleness.[2]

CHAPTER 4: COMMUNITY AND MISSION

To seek first God's kingdom and his righteousness is not an individualistic journey. By design in Scripture and by nature, we are meant to be part of a collective life. There are many variations of community—what I call *life together*. My understanding is that the early church didn't hold seminars to create mission statements about their common life. What happened was primarily the work of the Spirit in the newly born lives of those first converts, and yet even today there are principles and practicalities to experiencing community. It can be a long journey requiring much patience. There are spiritual truths we will never grasp and Christian standards we will never attain, except as we share in community with other believers. The Holy Spirit ministers to us, in large measure, through each other. We grow into community as we follow what God's Spirit is up to in our lives.

CHAPTER 5: WORSHIP AND DEVOTION

Vibrant, creative, and Spirit-empowered worship is a vital expression of Matt 6:33. In Luke chapter 4 when Jesus was tempted to receive all kingdoms of the world by worshiping Satan, he responded by saying his chief goal was to worship and serve God. Life and ministry can be ordinary. We cannot always live or worship on highs; thus the value of thoughtful liturgy. At times when worship is so alive, we can be helped to a fresh openness to God. Worship can then be transformative. There are three fallacies that can be made about public worship, namely that it is about *place*, about *form*, or about *us*. To understand worship is to see it in the paradigm of the rainbow or kaleidoscope: multicolored, multifaceted, and open to a range of possibilities and expressions. I will share my excitement about Isa 6:1–9 on the vitality of worship. What we are (or are not) in private worship spills over into what we do in public.

---

2. Willard, *Allure of Gentleness*, 1.

Preview of Topics

CHAPTER 6: LEADERSHIP AND CHARACTER

Leadership is dependent on the character of those leading. Culture and nurture have something to do with the formation of character, but it also formed by the choices we make in life. We all experience failure in our lives, one way or the other. We need accountability and camaraderie to sustain us in integrity. I will tell several stories about leadership, which are meant to show that the task of a leader is not to create a system that *governs* but one that *empowers*. Functional leadership is about making others able to share ministry and to equip them for service. This mindset about leadership flows out of an understanding that the church is a body composed of the priesthood of all believers. Paul reminds us that every church community has the resources to carry out its mission. Leaders are to discern God's gifts in others and, according to Eph 4:11–16, stir them to love and good works. We seek first the kingdom and its righteousness when we offer affirming and empowering leadership in whatever realm we are called.

EPILOGUE: INTO AN INCREASINGLY TROUBLED WORLD

There are so many challenges and fears that are happening in our world today. As we seek first his kingdom in our everyday lives, I conclude the book by sharing four principles that have come to matter most to me and have been my guide as to how to live righteously.
I think we are called to live:

- truthfully (people of integrity)
- hopefully (pointing the way)
- compassionately (caring for hurts and struggles)
- dialogically (listening to one another with empathy and understanding)

CHAPTER 1

Entering the Kingdom

No ear may hear His coming, but in this world of sin,
Where meek souls will receive Him still, the dear Christ enters in.
—"O Little Town of Bethlehem," by Bishop Phillips Brooks[1]

To "seek first his kingdom and his righteousness" (Matt 6:33), which is the theme of this book, leads me to share stories of what I understand initiation into that kingdom to be. There is no one template for how this comes about. All kinds of people, writers, musicians, philosophers, artists, et al., are initiated in the kingdom in so many ways, and in doing so do not express their experience like mine. There are devout believers who cannot pinpoint a specific time and place in which they became citizens of God's kingdom.

The good news about the kingdom is that God has broken into history, including our own personal history. *He broke into mine.* That story is the main thrust of this chapter. I believe that entering God's kingdom is primarily a spiritual and psychological experience that comes from the sovereignty and mystery of God more than the human intellect. The gospel is about what God has done, and that ought to be the main testimony however we enter the kingdom.

---

1. Brooks, "O Little Town," stanza 3.

Kingdom First

STORIES

My Entry into the Kingdom

I was born in Liverpool, England, made famous by the Beatles. The movie *Yesterday*[2] affords an entertaining glimpse of who they were and the setting in which I was raised. I grew up during the Second World War (1939–1945) in a poor area close to Anfield, the soccer stadium of the Liverpool Football Club. I did not know my father until he returned from the Second World War, when I was almost seven years old.

At the age of ten, a significant event happened. I passed what was called the "scholarship exam." Under the English educational system at the time, this exam was a means of streaming children into various levels of education for their teen years. The highest level was grammar school, which could eventually lead to university entrance.

An assembly was held one morning near the close of the school year at the elementary school which I attended. Among the usual school prize-giving and sports rewards came the significant and much-anticipated announcement of those who had passed the scholarship entrance into grammar school. It was where a high level of education was offered and paid for by the state. Among the three hundred and fifty pupils in that assembly, only two names were read out; mine was one of them. Thereupon began the journey into a new world, quite out of character for myself and the neighborhood in which I lived.

I was accepted as a pupil to the Liverpool Collegiate Institute. More recently, when asked to describe a grammar school to my North American friends, I facetiously suggested that it is much like the first of the Harry Potter movies, *Harry Potter and the Sorcerer's Stone*, minus the flying broomsticks of Hogwarts.[3] If I want to get more serious, I refer to *Tom Brown's Schooldays*, a novel by Thomas Hughes. (This novel may perk the interest of Rugby players and fans for it was at the grammar school in Rugby, England, that the game of rugby was born.)

It was at the Liverpool Collegiate that I experienced the very best of an English (high) school education that a working-class lad from a poor socioeconomic area would not normally have known. Those years were so formative in my life. They were designed by God to prepare me for his future for my life in the kingdom. In that setting was my form (class) teacher

2. Boyle, *Yesterday*.
3. Columbus, *Harry Potter*.

for five years, Richard Darton (an Oxford University scholar), who must have been directed by God to keep an eye on one of his troublesome pupils. Near the end of my time at Liverpool Collegiate, he took me aside and said, "Roxburgh, you are searching. You will not find what you seek except in Jesus Christ."

Weeks later at the end of term, while camping with four school buddies from the Liverpool Collegiate, I was confronted by a church group who were on holiday nearby. The four of us lads were asleep that Sunday morning in our tent, having been out to the local village pub the night before. Suddenly a soccer ball hit the tent, woke me up, and I rushed out. There before me was a group of about twenty teenage young people. They were part of a church that was holding a weeklong conference at the YMCA camp just up the hill.

A very pretty girl in the group looked straight at me and said, "Would you like to come to church?" An hour later, I and one other of our camping quartet went up to their meeting. My motive for going was the pretty girl who had issued the invitation. At the meeting I heard the story of the prodigal son as told in Luke 15. It was there and then, just before lunch, that I entered into the kingdom of God, as I identified with the prodigal son who, coming to his senses after a sense of loss, wanted to return home to his father.[4]

A week before I had gone on that camping trip, I watched a news report on television about the American evangelist, Billy Graham. I felt negative about him and was dismissive. When I returned from camping as a new believer, I saw another TV interview with Billy Graham in which he spoke of attending Wheaton College in Illinois. In my emotion and naivety, I told myself I would go there one day. Six years later I arrived at Wheaton

---

4. Jesus continued: "There was a man who had two sons. The younger one said to his father, 'Father, give me my share of the estate.' So he divided his property between them. Not long after that, the younger son got together all he had, set off for a distant country and there squandered his wealth in wild living. After he had spent everything, there was a severe famine in that whole country, and he began to be in need. So he went and hired himself out to a citizen of that country, who sent him to his fields to feed pigs. He longed to fill his stomach with the pods that the pigs were eating, but no one gave him anything. When he came to his senses, he said, 'How many of my father's hired servants have food to spare, and here I am starving to death! I will set out and go back to my father and say to him: Father, I have sinned against heaven and against you. I am no longer worthy to be called your son; make me like one of your hired servants.' So he got up and went to his father. But while he was still a long way off, his father saw him and was filled with compassion for him; he ran to his son, threw his arms around him and kissed him." (Luke 15:11–24)

College. I graduated from there in 1965, by which time I had married Brenda, and our first son, Cameron, had been born.

A few months after my conversion, I went to visit Richard Darton, my form teacher at the Collegiate, and told him of my commitment. He was deeply moved. Here was a man who loved me when it was so hard for others to do the same. There was more about the Liverpool Collegiate that shaped me. It included scholarly teachers and men of character who, despite my generally shallow behavior, earned my respect.

The school is now closed, but the magnificent building that housed it still exists and has been put to other use. I still have clear memories of assembly worship before the day of classes began. It was held in the great hall that had a magnificent pipe organ to accompany the hymns we sang each morning. (It is hard to believe now that this was not a religious school, but this was simply part of the old English grammar school culture.) It has been one of the shrines that I have revisited over these many years. I have returned to Liverpool often.

Just a few years ago, I went with my wife, Brenda, on a cruise around Britain. One phase of the journey sailed from Dublin to Liverpool. As the ship came into port on the River Mersey with its famous landscape of the Liver building, I stood on the forward deck (reminiscent of a scene from the movie *Titanic*) while the music of the Beatles was being played loudly throughout the ship. On the port side was the city and the Anglican cathedral, located near the Liverpool Collegiate. Not far away was the street where I was born.

On the starboard side of the ship, in the distance across the River Mersey, was a district called Wallasey. This was a more rural setting leading to the River Dee and the mountains of Wales. It was there, while camping in a little village called Barnston Dale, that I had been *born again*. I recognized this in a flood of joyful tears there on the boat deck that day.

> I heard the voice of Jesus say,
> "Behold, I freely give
> The living water; thirsty one,
> Stoop down, and drink, and live."
> I came to Jesus, and I drank
> of that life-giving stream;
> My thirst was quenched, my soul revived,
> And now I live in him.[5]

---

5. Bonar, "I Heard the Voice," verse 2.

Entering the Kingdom

INSIGHTS

Dual Citizenship

I emigrated to Canada in 1956 from the United Kingdom. I now hold dual citizenship as most immigrants do. They live in a different country from their birthplace and may even speak a different language. This presents difficulties at times, and the second generation is often torn between old and new values, as well as peer pressure. The same is true for children raised as second-generation Christians to parents who understood and lived the kingdom life. The pressures of the secular kingdom are enormous. As Christians, we also hold a form of dual citizenship, and so we are often confronted by two lifestyles. Believers live in a society whose values may not line up with the new life created in us when we join the kingdom of God. We accept this reality, but we must learn to do so as Jesus said, by seeking first his kingdom and his righteousness. We must love the neighborhood where we live and identify with much of its life while at the same time knowing that by virtue of the kingdom we serve, we have received a different mindset about our purpose in life.

In chapter 3, we will look at what it means to live in two worlds: the world of our friends and neighbors, as well as that of being citizens of God's kingdom. In this chapter, I have told the story of my entering into that second world by becoming a citizen of the kingdom of God.

POINTS TO PONDER

A vital part of living effectively as a Christian community is recovering the importance of a personal commitment to Christ and his influence and guidance in our everyday lives—at home, in our social life, and in our church ministries.

Everyone in the church needs a mindset that grasps that the Christian life is not just about church attendance. Instead, it is all about this truth expressed by Peter (I insert the passage here so that one can pause and meditate on its power):

> Praise be to the God and Father of our Lord Jesus Christ! In his great mercy he has given us new birth into a living hope through the resurrection of Jesus Christ from the dead, and into an inheritance that can never perish, spoil or fade. This inheritance is kept in heaven for you, who through faith are shielded by God's power until the coming of the salvation that is ready to be revealed in the last

time. In all this you greatly rejoice, though now for a little while you may have had to suffer grief in all kinds of trials. These have come so that the proven genuineness of your faith—of greater worth than gold, which perishes even though refined by fire—may result in praise, glory and honor when Jesus Christ is revealed. Though you have not seen him, you love him; and even though you do not see him now, you believe in him and are filled with an inexpressible and glorious joy, for you are receiving the end result of your faith, the salvation of your souls. (1 Pet 1:3–9)

On entering this kingdom, we become new people: people who are indwelt by the Holy Spirit. I deem this to be foundational because presenting our *beliefs* to neighbors has little impact until we present to them our *transformed lives*. The Liverpool neighborhood in which I lived knew something had happened to me in the months following my return from camping in Barnston Dale that weekend in August.

Beyond Self

In an age that puts an emphasis on emotions, we need to help people understand that commitment to Christ and to a life of seeking first his kingdom is not primarily about feelings or personal experience. In the months that followed my conversion, I grew in my understanding that the kingdom of God was to be my worldview. Little by little, I grasped that this kingdom was the spotlight shining in the dark, showing me how to live in the world. It gave me belonging and purpose as well as my sense of identity as a fellow citizen with other believers. I began to understand the fact that God has a plan for the restoration of all things and that I was privileged to be included in that overall plan. The biblical understanding of salvation is not merely that our lives will be set right again. It is that our lives are ushered into that which is greater than ourselves to participate in God's saving purpose and plan for the world. The gospel is primarily about God and only secondarily about us.

For Others

Astronaut James Erwin is one of the first humans to land on the moon. He visited us at Millmead Church in England once, and he signed a poster, which I hung in my office. He wrote, "What is more important than man walking on the moon is that God should walk on earth."

Entering the Kingdom

Alas, it is often a reality that our excitement can dry up, and we lose heart and desire. July 1 is Canada Day. There are many activities, and most days end with a fireworks show "downtown." When we first moved to Kelowna, Brenda and I went with my daughter, Heather, and her family to such a fireworks display. One had to go early to get a decent viewing spot of the fireworks that are often displayed from the lake, so Brenda and I did just that. It was a long time before the show began as hundreds pushed by us to find a place to sit. I watched them all drift in, people of every background and color, many new immigrants, young and old, as well as all levels of socioeconomic standing in life. The fireworks were shown, and once they ended people began drifting home. I sat there for a long time and Brenda wondered why I wasn't getting up to head home. I had been very quiet—not my usual self. With a lump in my throat, I turned to her and said, "Brenda, I have watched all this tonight, all these crowds, and have come to realize that while God so loved the world, I don't think that I do." I had lost the spirit of the Savior who I had come to love so much in the stories of this chapter. Growing older, wearying of church work, losing touch with God's Spirit, and neglecting prayer had all taken their toll on my zest. Thankfully, it returned over the next few months.

The Christian Celts of the fifth to the ninth centuries did not have target audiences. They had dynamic communities into which they invited the outsiders of their day to join them. My brother, Alan Roxburgh, so wisely said, "I wonder how many evangelism programs we would need if we simply practised hospitality with our neighbors." Our mission in our locality is to help others discover how God is already at work among them. We can encourage them to recognize and follow what he has already put in their heart.

I remember driving home from Calgary to my home in Kelowna. En route I was to speak in Vernon. The day had been long. I was heading to Vernon when I sensed God's Spirit prod me to stop in a little place called Enderby. I knew it and so protested to God that I had better things to do. Reluctantly, I went into Enderby and sat at a picnic table by the river. I took out my notes for my talk and was reviewing them when a "gang" of about a dozen teenagers, all unkempt, some on drugs, approached me. I thought I was in danger. They asked me what I was doing. I said I was studying. They asked about what, and I replied, "God." The leader of the group seemed calmer and more reasonable than the others. He said they didn't know anything about God. I asked if I could explain. He said yes, and I sat around a couple of tables with them and told the story of the prodigal son in Luke 15—the same story I had heard on the day of my conversion in Barnston.

We all talked back and forth for about an hour; some were interested, others were not. It was approaching time for me to get to Vernon, which was about twenty-five kilometers down the road. The leader looked at me and said, "Thank You, mister. We walk around here a lot, and no one your age even looks at us. They just pass by on the other side." This struck me as reminiscent of the good Samaritan story and what the religious people had done to the man fallen by the side of the road. My talk that night in Vernon took on new life because I had not passed by on the other side.

Many of you reading my stories have similar ones of your own. Like you, I have had unique and diverse times when I was able to share my faith simply because God's Spirit prompted me to do so. Here are two more stories that give me joy to tell.

One day I was traveling by ferry to Victoria, British Columbia, when I got talking to a lawyer about this and that. Before we docked, we agreed to do lunch sometime. That began a series of lunches near his office. After several months he asked me if I could tell him how to consider Christianity. I said that I would gladly do that, but it would cost him a lot of money (my Liverpool humor again). I said that he should book an afternoon at his office for us to talk together. For a lawyer to do that would really be an economic cost. That afternoon came, and after a couple of hours he decided to be a follower of Jesus. He and his wife were baptized some months later.

The other story relates to my time when, in "retirement," I was being a consultant to a church on the east coast of England that had gone through difficulties. (I did several such assignments, both in Canada and England, during this "retirement" period.) Right on the North Sea coast was a quaint restaurant that I claimed as my "office" during my months at the church. I did this in order to meet people away from the formal church building environment. I consumed many cups of tea over many conversations. (Very early every Sunday morning, I would have devotions there, look over my sermon, and then over breakfast read the *Sunday Times* or the *Observer* newspapers before heading to church to preach.) For several weeks, I had been connected by a church leader to a young woman who, with her boyfriend, was heavily into drugs and other problems. She asked if we could talk one day. I suggested we meet in my "office." We did, and for two wonderful hours we talked together, and she committed her life to Jesus. Beneath almost every pained and struggling life is what Augustine wrote about in his book *Confessions*: "We also carry our mortality about with us, carry the evidence of our sin.... You [God] arouse us so that praising you may bring us joy, because you have made us and drawn us to yourself, and our heart is restless until it rests in you."[6]

I have returned to that "sacred" little restaurant several times since, sat with a cup of tea looking out toward the beach and the North Sea, and choked up as I remembered the day in which that young woman entered the kingdom. Her boyfriend soon came to the same decision, and they both went on to gain biblical training. Both now provide leadership in ministries of social compassion as they live for the kingdom of God.

Many devout believers may feel intimidated by a world that has developed so much indifference or antagonism to institutionalized Christianity. A study I once read indicated that only 10 percent of church members are evangelists. I can accept that—along with the biblical fact that 100 percent are meant to be witnesses. Paul made it clear that some sow, some water, but God gives the increase. I am not advocating for sets of formulas or programs about witnessing, but we need to help each other participate in common activities where together we can live out our faith before others. This is our common task, not a specialized endeavor for a few. There is power in personal stories of faith. We are not witnessing to a set of beliefs, doctrines, or any particular expression of Christianity but to our experience of Jesus. John tells the lovely story of how Andrew sought out Peter in order to introduce him to Jesus.[7] Sometimes we can do what Andrew did for Peter or what the pretty teenage girl did for me that morning at Barnston Camp when she asked me if I wanted to "come to church."

The rest of this book seeks to share that Matt 6:33 can be lived out, not as some fiat but as a natural expression of the transforming experience revealed in the stories above.

APPENDIX

Books

- C. S. Lewis, *Surprised by Joy: The Shape of My Early Life*

---

6. Crossroads Initiative, "Our Heart."
7. John 1:35–42.

The book is a memoir that explores Lewis's journey from atheism to Christianity, detailing the "surprising" moments of joy that he experienced along the way. It offers a unique perspective on faith and personal transformation.[8]

- John M. Mulder and Hugh Thomson Kerr, *Finding God: A Treasury of Conversion Stories*

Ranging from the first century to the present, *Finding God* is a digest of conversion stories from a wide variety of people—from the apostle Paul to the rock musician Bono. These narratives demonstrate the remarkable diversity of spiritual journeys and the dramatic changes that can result from encounters with God.[9]

- Verlon Fosner, *Dinner Church: Building Bridges by Breaking Bread*

Inviting someone to a dinner at which Jesus is explained and his life shared is a very different thing than inviting them to a worship/teaching event on a Sunday morning in the average church. Fosner shares with us how adapting the early church's habit of meeting and sharing around meals transformed his Seattle community. In the early days of the Christian church, such meetings tended to involve, in simple ways, telling the stories of Jesus. Fosner's book helps us to understand the importance of people experiencing a life-changing encounter with Jesus Christ.[10]

My daughter, Heather, is the pastoral leader at a new church plant called The Gathering in West Kelowna, British Columbia. She is helping form a dinner church that can creatively serve the neighborhood and model to it the kingdom of God.

- Leonard Sweet, *From Tablet to Table: Where Community Is Found and Identity Is Formed*

Sweet emphasizes the importance of eating together at home, at church, and in the world where we can display the hospitality of God. Both Sweet and Fosner are pointing out that the pulpit-pew mindset of much Christian activity falls short of our reaching people in ways to which they can readily relate.[11]

---

8. Lewis, *Surprised by Joy*, 15.
9. Mulder and Kerr, *Finding God*.
10. Fosner, *Dinner Church*.
11. Sweet, *From Tablet to Table*.

CHAPTER 2

Kingdom and the Church

And I tell you that you are Peter, and on this rock I will build my church, and the gates of Hades will not overcome it.

—Matthew 16:18

Church is not a place to which you go but a family to which you belong.[1]

CHURCH IS A VITAL aspect of Christian community; it is bedrock to the growth of our lives as believers, and it is foundational to a life of seeking first the kingdom of God. The form of a gathering is less important to me than its *life together* in the world, of which believers are an integral a part. Regardless of the struggles of today's church in the West, by living out Matt 6:33, we will find meaning and fulfillment together as God's people.

STORIES

A Place to Belong

The immediate days that followed my conversion involved me cycling thirty-five miles (fifty-five kilometers) early each Sunday morning to travel from Liverpool to Manchester to the church of the young people who had first introduced me to Christ. My bike rides each week meant I worshiped

---

1. Warren, "Church Family."

in the morning with these folk, went to Sunday school in the afternoon, and then attended the evening service and young peoples' meeting before getting back on my bike for the long ride back home to Liverpool in the dark. I didn't just "attend church" in those months, I found a place to belong. I was discovering that church was an integral part of becoming a citizen of the kingdom. Winter set in, and then I discovered friends at a small Baptist Church in Liverpool that was composed mostly of the same age group that had led me to Christ in the summer. They had a vibrant faith and a desire to share it in several creative ways.

I was baptized and became a member at the Orrell Park Baptist Church in Liverpool. The next two years remain among the most exhilarating of my life, and they gave me such a deep experience of community as well as lifelong friends. Two summers after my conversion, I went with these young church folk to a Christian retreat center named Hildenborough Hall in Frinton, on the southeast coast of England. It was led by Tom and Dick Rees, Anglican ministers. At the end of the week, we all gathered in a thirteenth-century, little Anglican church at midnight; there I sensed a call to ministry. I went out to the beach alone and walked for a long time with the North Sea waters near my footsteps. There I felt impressed by God to emigrate to Canada to prepare for some form of Christian ministry. I knew that given my life's circumstances at the time, such a move would facilitate my further education and training.

Getting on a plane to Canada was somewhat of a miracle. The year was 1956. It was the time of the so-called Suez Canal Crisis when Britain invaded Egypt. As a result, thousands were emigrating from England to Australia, South Africa, Kenya, and Canada at a rapid pace. I went to the Canadian emigration office to seek permission to go to Canada. The official kindly told me I didn't have a chance, but even if I did it would take up to two years. I had no sponsor, no trade, no money; that didn't help my application.

I went back to the Canadian office every week and pestered them (as well as praying at home). On one such visit, the official asked me why I was being so persistent. In my innocence I simply said, "God has told me to go to Canada to study for the ministry." He looked at me, took my application form, stamped it, and said, "Go." I received the acceptance papers in the mail a week or so later. The major odds and hurdles had been overcome, but that was not the end of the saga. All along I kept wondering how I would get the money to pay for my flight. My sister had recently settled in Winnipeg,

Kingdom and the Church

and she and her husband, with a new baby, couldn't afford the funds. My parents were relatively poor. In those days, there were no credit cards or GoFundMe projects. I had only my simple trust in God to provide.[2]

I received a letter from my sister, Jean, that Air Canada had just initiated a new plan called "Go Now Pay Later." She and her husband would sponsor me for the fare, for which I had two years to pay back to Air Canada. I landed in Winnipeg in late November of 1956. My journey had entered a new stage. Through all the circumstances of my life that have followed since then, I have always lived with the question "Why me?" because I am somewhat overwhelmed by God's grace.[3]

In Winnipeg, I joined Elim Chapel on Portage Avenue, which was closely associated with InterVarsity Christian Fellowship at that time. In the short year that I was there, I got to know Bill Mason, the well-known author of *Paddle to the Sea*, which is the story of a remarkable journey made by a toy canoe based on Bill's knowledge of and ability in canoeing. During that spring and summer, Bill took me under his wing and taught me to canoe properly. That was an invaluable gift.

I began this chapter with a simple story of my entry into church life born out of my excitement. Eventually, I entered into church leadership with its inevitable ups and downs, joys and struggles. One constant of my journey, wherever I served, was that I felt deeply committed to my Lord and his church, whatever was going on and whatever were my personal shortcomings.

This next anecdote comes from the time I was working through my master of divinity degree at Winnipeg University's School of Theology. The class was dealing with a historic survey of local churches. The professor told us a story from many years earlier. He was teaching a class in 1939 and was relaying to his students his sadness over the closing of First Baptist Church Winnipeg. Due to its inner-city location, it had continued to lose members until it could no longer sustain its ministry. A student in class popped up and said that they shouldn't be discouraged because the Pentecostals had bought the building, and it was now packed out every Sunday. That was the founding of Calvary Temple in Winnipeg, which developed over the years into the large and significant ministry that is still in that city today.

---

2. "And my God will meet all your needs according to the riches of his glory in Christ Jesus" (Phil 4:19).

3. "The grace of our Lord was poured out on me abundantly, along with the faith and love that are in Christ Jesus" (1 Tim 1:14).

(First Baptist Church amalgamated with Broadway Baptist and still has a ministry in their new location.)

Sincerity Not Enough

A few years ago, I visited Edinburgh, Scotland. I took time to revisit the city since I had spent part of my early childhood, during World War II, not many miles away. Downtown is known for its three hills, one on which stands Edinburgh Castle, another Carlton Hill, and the other named Arthur's Seat, on the top of which are panoramic views of Edinburgh and the land stretching out to the North Sea.

One early morning I walked by road to the top of Arthur's Seat, enjoyed the vistas, and took time to meditate. As I started to go back down the hill, I came across a group of sincere men praying in a quiet corner. The intent of their prayers was laudable. The topic of their prayers was misplaced. They were, with genuine piety, asking God to restore the former glory of the city's religious life and heritage. They wanted God to fill the famous churches that were located downtown and restore the spirituality of the mid-twentieth-century life. However, since their prayers were all about restoring what they knew from the past, it all seemed like a good dose of nostalgia and misplaced desire.

Princes Street, the renowned strip of shops, hotels, gardens, museums, and churches, still had much traditional Scots flavor. The evening before my trip up Arthur's Seat, I walked beyond Princes Street to the different world of George Street and Rose Street, where the younger set visited bistros and discos, etc. I talked to them over snacks and coffee in places like Hard Rock Café. Their accents were still Scottish but with a more European flavor. They had little interest in church but were open to spiritual conversation.

I admired the men up the top of Arthur's Seat who were praying for the city with earnestness that morning, but they lacked the insight about what was going on in the city and knew not how to discern what God was up to in their rapidly changing community.

INSIGHTS

I love the church and write with empathy for what in my life has been a home. From the first days of my conversion, the church became to me a place of an extended family, and most often its fellowship offered me significance and self-worth. Like most marriages, down through the years there have been high points and low points in my church life, but as the covenant I made on my wedding day remains, so in a similar vogue I intend to stay loyal to God's people and Christ's kingdom.

There are varying sides to the understanding of what is going on in church around the world. A host of contemporary writers who are critiquing the church and envisioning a whole new way of understanding what our life together ought to be have great value, and we do well to heed them. Socrates said that the unexamined life was not worth living; the same can be said for the church. Examination in and of itself, however, is not enough. There are deep issues for church leaders to face and with which to deal. We must keep our eyes and hearts open to what God is saying to the church while at the same time living out Matt 6:33 in our individual and corporate lives.

Struggles

Most of the authors I have read who critique the church have no desire or intent to abandon it. I am not blind to the effect of both secularism in the culture and obscurantism among Christians on the church's image and its resulting rejection by many. The church will always have certain institutional aspects, but it is not primarily an institution—it is a fellowship of the Holy Spirit. Whatever the form of church, whatever our expression, we must know that we are called to a place of belonging among a group of fellow strugglers who are attempting to keep in step with the Spirit right in the thick of a secular culture, looking for signs of the kingdom at work. We are not to be mere consumers of all the amenities that church has to offer each week, such as sermons, worship groups, and all kinds of programs, however good they may be. As a genuine community, we are to be primarily about the mission of Jesus, who said that he had come to seek and to save the lost, and to participate in the extension of his kingdom.

Different Expressions

I have taken only a few cruise ship holidays in my life, but one in particular comes to mind. It was aboard the *Ruby Princess* in the fall of 2013. One early morning at dawn, I sat in a remote section of the top deck and pondered all that I had experienced of the church in my life and the scores of books that I had read. I wrote for several hours. Here is a small part of what I wrote:

Kingdom First

The church is clearly a very important part of the kingdom of God, but we need to be looking for a fresh way in which believers are to live incarnationally in their culture, sharing a comprehensive gospel, modeling how to seek first the kingdom of God and his righteousness.

Such a quest will not be about finding the right way to do church or about fixing what we have now, but about the fact that it is our task to find out what God is up to in the culture and how the culture at times may even be expressing the kingdom of God in some instances or localities in ways that we have not ourselves conceived. We will need a different imagination about what the church is and what is the importance of the kingdom.

Western churches will continue for a time, just like ethnic churches do in immigrant settings, but eventually new forms of expression (likely also within historic liturgical churches) will be created by believers seeking to live in the new world they are experiencing.

We can only speak of going on a pilgrimage of discovery to hear the mind of God and the outworkings of his kingdom in this new culture. This will take a lot of listening and hard thinking. We will need patience, *for there will be many struggles along the way. We will need humility. To suggest that a new breed of "clergy/leaders" are going to do it better by some new approach is both naive and arrogant. I doubt that there will be any new Luther, Calvin, Billy Graham, or any such great charismatic figures to show the way, nor even a particular model of church (of which there are now so many); but instead, I think God will use a plethora of ordinary leaders connecting through networks, sharing what they are discovering with each other in a local town or community. We will need* openness *to the mind and life of the Spirit, as well as a lot of* risk-taking *and even* rejection. *Whatever will emerge may only evolve through decades of struggle. Church fads and quick fixes have wearied us for too long. What seems certain to me is that the church we have known since even the Reformation does not represent "the" only way to express gospel and kingdom but rather "a" way. Renewal, awakenings, and fresh reformations will open churches to whatever new forms are led by the Spirit.*

A Marginalized Church

To most in society, church is no longer a place of truth, belonging, comfort, or guidance. This has left so many adrift. Many church members, while they "do church" faithfully and sincerely, may not know the real heart of what the gospel was intended to be or how the kingdom of God was meant to be expressed in a living community that goes deeper than just "doing church."

God is still at work, and it is his view that the church, as part of the kingdom, will prevail, but we need fresh understandings. The church is in difficult times. It has been marginalized by the culture, pushed from the front seat to the back seat. To understand the disappearing influence of Christians in the West, one must realize that the church is no longer at the center of things, and the culture has devalued it. Instead of trying to recapture the past or return the church to a place of status, Christians need to realize that the way they have been functioning for so long is failing to relate. No matter what kind of church Christians attend on a Sunday—large, small, traditional, creative, discouraged, excited, or whatever—they all come out after their meeting into a world that at best ignores them, is indifferent to them, or has no real connection with them.

I realize that, seemingly in contradiction to what I have written above, there are cultural movements that create megachurches. The United States has almost fifteen hundred megachurches (those with over two thousand in attendance each week). There are other megachurches that exist in several countries such as Sub-Saharan Africa, South America, and parts of Asia and Europe, including the United Kingdom. Some of these churches have a vast effect on the political mindset of those who attend. Some have failed, but others have succeeded and continue to multiply. Most are led by unique individuals. One needs to know the ethnic and cultural history that undergirds these movements and to understand the context in which they emerge if we are to keep perspective. These churches will not fade any time soon. We need also to acknowledge that some megachurches of various denominations emerge because of a movement of God's Spirit and a faithfulness to the vision of God's kingdom; such churches are making a wonderful impact on their communities in terms of mission, social endeavor, and the worship of God. It is important for us also to note that megachurches represent less than 2 percent of all church attendees worldwide. The majority of churches in the West number under one hundred and fifty in attendance each week. There is also a significant growth of so-called house churches in their many varied expressions. Their attendance numbers each week are quite small by nature of where they meet, but some form a network of such gatherings with a common overall leadership team.

The decline and erosion of the church in the West is well documented. The Missional Church movement, about which so many scholarly books have been written and so many projects have been launched, has not changed this situation. Despair over analysis and criticism is not what is needed. God's kingdom and Christ's teaching about the church causes me to look for hope, and I want to give encouragement. Whatever our perception of the church, we need the humility to grasp that we all have such a narrow view of what is really going on in the kingdom at large. We need to heed the words that Hamlet once said to Horatio, "There are more things on heaven and earth, Horatio, / Than are dreamt of in your philosophy."[4] We should believe in, pray for, and work for the renewal of churches we know that are struggling. We need a humble crying out to God to show us the way for our day. We can only speak of going on a pilgrimage of discovery to hear the mind of God and the outworkings of his kingdom in this new culture.[5]

Encouragement and Care

There are still "good news" churches (Christian communities) everywhere in the world. Many churches do significant kingdom work that needs to be praised. Within their context they are providing for spiritual growth, meaningful worship, community, and mission. At their best, these churches have recognized that their challenge is to have a deep engagement with the ways in which the gospel transforms people's lives. I know or hear about genuine pastors and leaders who, even in these troubled times, love God and seek to lead the churches to which they are called with integrity and care for others. They have a grasp of the gospel and seek to guide members into a faithful expression of the kingdom in their own context. They help them understand that church is not a place to which you go, but a family to which you belong. They are opening up to the problem of clergy-dominated congregational life and are themselves evolving to a less dominant, more inclusive expression of leadership.

---

4. Shakespeare, *Hamlet*, act 1, scene 5, lines 187–88.

5. Martin Robinson and Alan Roxburgh, in part of their book give us a historical sketch of how the church got to be where it seems to be today. The book "speaks to the bewilderment and helplessness many churches feel in the face of current events.... Throughout its history, the church has faced crises of meaning and identity in all kinds of changing contexts. The crises facing the churches of the western hemisphere today are no different." Roxburgh and Robinson, *Practices*, back cover.

Kingdom and the Church

Alas, there are also many who, despite their sincerity and hard work, feel defeated about congregational life and the things they are called upon to do that bear little resemblance to genuine kingdom issues. They are not sure where to turn. Some churches and their leaders are feeling hopeless. They were trained to lead in a world that no longer fits where society has gone and will continue to go. They are exhausted by trying to "fix" the church or deal with congregations that seem but a shadow of an earlier vitality and desire for mission. It's time to turn in a new direction because not much seems to be working anymore. It would be wrong to discount the efforts of these struggling and discouraged churches and their leaders. It is churlish to discount or dismiss these facts about faithful people. Instead, they need encouragement and help considering the questions they are asking. I hope to further these ideas in chapter 6, and I make some suggestions in the appendix at the end of that chapter.

My son Cameron is lead pastor at The Neighbourhood Church in Vancouver (formerly Southside Community Church). From its inception under his leadership over thirty years ago, it has continually lived out its goal of living incarnationally in their neighborhood, using many creative and caring ways. It recently embarked on an ambitious project to transform its institutional building and expand it in a significant neighborhood project that will provide social, cultural, and artistic amenities as well as low-cost housing. This is not new or unique, of course; many churches have done this over decades and will continue to do so in the future. Another example in a very different Christian tradition is First United Church on Hastings Street in Vancouver, British Columbia, ministering as it does to scores of human needs among street people. In the UK, a group called Street Pastors uses volunteers to do similar work. There are so many churches that do care, that haven't given up, that are enjoying the favor of all the people, and being effective in their setting. The last thing these churches and leaders search for is some new method; rather they want help, relationships, and to find a new hope.[6]

The world has so dramatically changed for the church in society since I took that immigrant flight to Canada long ago. The present journey is different in many ways and will be difficult, but we must keep seeking first his kingdom because Christ urged us to do so. We must also continue to believe in his word to Peter based on his faith: "On this rock I will build my church" (Matt 16:18).

---

6. In the book *When Church Stops Working*, authors Andrew Root and Blair D. Bertrand also stress what I have noted above, namely the need not to look for new methods or structures but to wait on God and reflect on what he wants us to do.

POINTS TO PONDER

There seems to be no particular model of church that is the right approach, so whether we are surrounded by struggling or successful churches, we need to be seeking God to help us bloom where we are planted by applying Matt 6:33 to all of our lives and by being who we are as people who love Jesus.

In John 21, when the resurrected Christ had breakfast on the shore of Galilee with his disciples, he had that well-known talk with Peter in which he asked, "Peter, do you love me?" Part of that conversation includes Christ's response to Peter's question about John in verses 20–21: "Lord what about him?" Jesus' response is curt: "What is that to you? You must follow me" (John 21:22).

Church models abound, and as I indicated earlier, criticizing them or trying to copy them is futile. Rather, we need to be on a long journey to a new and Spirit-inspired transformation in our own church community. Wise leaders will start from where they are at present. Brave leaders will listen to the Spirit. (I suggest ways in chapter 6 as to how this might be experienced.)

APPENDIX

Leadership Help

There are numerous organizations and movements around the world that have wrestled with the issues of the church and have made some important and hopeful discoveries that can be of significant help to any who are seeking a way forward. There are many others, but here are few that I know.

Organizations

- The Missional Network, founded by Alan Roxburgh (themissionalnetwork.com)
- Gravity Leadership, founded by Ben Stenke and Matt Tebbe
- Commons Network, people joining with God in our neighborhoods (thecommonsnetwork.com)
- Fresh Expressions, founded by Steven Croft and Peter Pillinger (https://freshexpressions.com/training)
- Renovare, founded by Richard J. Foster (renovare.org)

- Parish Collectives, founded by Paul Sparks, Tim Soerens, and Dwight Friesen (parishcollective.org)
- Missional Church Network, Forge Kansas City, cofounded by Brad Brisco (www.missionalchurchnetwork.com)
- V3 Church Planting Movement. The V3 is part of a national groundswell of planters and practitioners that want to help start and sustain new churches (thev3movement.org)
- Missio-Alliance. This is a growing collection of various kinds of resources. The aim of all these resources is the promotion of further dialogue among Christian leaders and the equipping of the church (missioalliance.org)
- Missional International Church Network, founded by Warren Reeve
- Global Leadership Network (globalleadership.org)
- Forge Global (forge.teachable.com)
- The Pastorate Cohorts online (thepastorate.ca)
- Church Renewal International. This offers superb online mentoring for pastors (churchrenewal.com)

General Books

- Lesslie Newbigin, *The Household of God: Lectures on the Nature of Church*
- Avery Dulles, *Models of the Church*
- David Fitch, *What Is the Church and Why Does It Exist?*

Church Renewal Books

To choose so few out of so many books about church change was a very difficult task for me. It ended up being simply a matter of my judgment about contemporary church needs.

- Howard A. Snyder, *The Community of the King*
- Scot McKnight, *Kingdom Conspiracy: Returning to the Radical Mission of the Local Church*

- Alan J. Roxburgh, *Joining God in the Great Unraveling: Where We Are and What I've Learned*
- Mark Sayers, *Disappearing Church: From Cultural Relevance to Gospel Resilience*
- Andrew Root and Blair D. Bertrand, *When Church Stops Working: A Future for Your Congregation Beyond More Money, Programs, and Innovation*
- Les Biggs, *The Challenge of Understanding the Kingdom of God*[7]
- Stuart Murray, *Church After Christendom*
- Alan Hirsch, *The Forgotten Ways: Reactivating the Missional Church*
- Mark Buchanan, *Your Church Is Too Safe: Why Following Christ Turns the World Upside Down*

---

7. This dissertation can be obtained at Carey Theological College of Vancouver, British Columbia.

CHAPTER 3

A Tale of Two Cultures

My Kingdom is not of this world.

—JOHN 18:36

They are not of the world any more than I am of the world. My prayer is not that you take them out of the world but that you protect them from the evil one.

—JOHN 17:14–15

CHRISTIANS BELONG BOTH TO God's kingdom and to the world in which he has placed us. We need to be connected to and care for those who are in what colloquially is called the "secular" world. The strongest conviction that caused me to write this book was that in the last half century at least, Christians are being governed less by God's kingdom and more by the culture in which they were raised. I remember a particular pastoral situation in which a church member wanted to take another member to court over a minor legal issue. When I pointed out that in 1 Cor 6:1–8 Paul says we mustn't do that, he was dumfounded. He had adapted the mindset of a litigious culture. All our lives are governed to some degree by the world in which we were raised. It affects our thinking, habits, goals, values, priorities, and our attitude to others who are not like we are, either ethnically or politically. Jesus introduces us to the kingdom and to a whole new vision of life so that what is really important and true is brought to our focus.

Leaders (parents, pastors, et al.) need to teach that we are living in a world of often-competing values and that we are to seek first the kingdom (Matt 6:33) and thereby enter a different narrative of life, a different lens through which we see the world and how the Christian community operates.

The cultural demarcation lines cannot always be finely drawn. I lived for the first eighteen years of my life in Liverpool's working-class culture, which is quite unique and gave birth to the Beatles and their particular expression of life, both musically and philosophically. This had an enormous influence on shaping who I am, including my weird sense of humor. The subculture of life at Liverpool Collegiate had an even deeper effect on me, making me sensitive to English language and literature. Then came my decision to follow Jesus as I became part of God's kingdom. I entered the whole new world of what some call Christian counterculture. I didn't cast off the treasured parts of my past or give up my love for and ability in soccer, for example.

Ever since I became a citizen of the kingdom, I have lived with enthusiasm and fulfillment in the two worlds I mentioned above. This is how it was meant to be for God's people in his kingdom. The following stories and examples are likely not special or very different than those in which many believers engage. I insert them to simply illustrate the point that to seek first the kingdom of God is to be involved in two cultures while adhering to God's righteousness.

STORIES

Motorbikes

I have had motorcycles since I was eighteen years of age and only ceased to ride when I approached eighty. This hobby took me into many experiences in the world, especially when I joined a secular motorcycle club. I was asked to join a Christian motorcycle club, but I declined that option. The secular club provided much pleasure and camaraderie.

In the last few years, we met as a club every two weeks for breakfast and shared and swapped ideas about bikes and trips we were to make. These trips generally took place on weekends, and I would plan not to preach at my church when I went with them. When we did longer tours and rallies that took a week or so, I would generally set out to join up with them right after church on Sunday. That involved long and fast riding to catch up with them by Monday breakfast somewhere in the middle of nowhere. We would meet at a campsite and cook meals together, then sit around the campfire and drink and tell jokes, most of which were off-color. I always stayed around the campfire until about eleven o'clock at night and then went to bed. The next morning as I sat outside of my tent reading, almost inevitably someone would come to me and want to talk. They had issues and knew that I would listen. Then I would join the gang for breakfast before we went riding into the mountains, which could be both exciting and scary.

Like any club, they had socials at Christmas and at other times. I always went and had fun. We also attended motorcycle shows together. They were great people, and I let them know that I was proud to belong with them and ride as their friend. They knew I was a Christian, and whenever one of them or their relatives got cancer or a serious illness, they asked for my help. One day we all rode into the mountains where I performed a burial for one of the gang members whose brother had died. That was a different funeral indeed.

Soccer

I think I was born with soccer shoes already on. As I grew up, I played for both my high school and community teams. I played varsity at college, and then when I went into pastoral ministry, I played for secular teams in the towns where I lived—even for a semipro team in one place. I once played for an Italian team; they affectionately called me "the priest." As our family developed, I lived soccer vicariously through both our sons' involvement, where I coached, or through my lifetime support of Liverpool FC.

Suzuki Music

My wife, Brenda, has two music degrees from the Royal Conservatory of Music. Without negating her classical music education, she affirmed and became involved in what has been called the Suzuki method of music education, which stresses community association and involvement as a learning model. Certainly, this was a different culture than the motorcycle club. Suzuki music involved me following Brenda's leadership and joining with the whole family in much the same way as we all did when camping together over the years.

Dr. Suzuki, in his book *Nurtured by Love*, states the obvious, namely that Japanese children speak Japanese. It is one of the world's most difficult languages, but they learn it because they grow up in a Japanese-speaking home and society. As children, they are nurtured by love to imbibe Japanese. The philosophy of Suzuki music schools is that as children learn age-by-age and step-by-step in a context of everyone encouraging them and playing the same tunes with them at the same time in groups (as well as their individual lessons with a teacher), they simply imbibe what is being taught.[1] The opportunity to attend a weeklong Suzuki summer camp with one's family, and all the other students, afforded a child the chance to enhance his/her experience. I lived with Suzuki music culture for years and saw the effect of that on our children. In the same way, Brenda and I shared our kingdom values in our family life, and I have seen the effect of that on our children's spiritual lives to this day.

Politics

Brenda's father was a deputy mayor and city councillor for many years, as well as the president in the local county of the CCF Party (Co-operative Commonwealth Federation, the forerunner to the New Democratic Party in Canada). Her family, who lived in Oshawa, was deeply involved in politics during her growing up years. I, too, was always interested in politics and spent my time when I was in Winnipeg, for example, on the executive of the reelection committee for a national party cabinet minister. When I pastored in Vancouver, I arranged, along with a few other leaders, to have an interpolitical rally at the Agrodome in the Pacific National Exhibition grounds. The theme was to allow the leading lights in each party who were running for federal election to present their views from a Christian perspective. This they did this before about four hundred people. Tommy Douglas was at that time the leader of the New Democratic Party. He gave a fiery speech about what he termed "Christian Socialism." Because Brenda had known him and met with him and her father from time to time, we invited Tommy to dinner after the rally. That was a rewarding evening as we discussed issues with the man who Canadians voted in a national poll as the most significant Canadian leader of the last hundred years. In his prepolitical years, he had been a Baptist pastor.

---

1. Suzuki, *Nurtured by Love*.

Tommy Douglas came from an era in which leaders of several political persuasions worked together in genuine altruism. They were civil and respectful of one another. I am saddened that we have now become in North America so polarized over politics to the point where we live fractious lives instead of working together for the common good.

Service Clubs

When I lived in the United States, I belonged to the Jaycees, and in Canada to Kiwanis and Probus service clubs.

"Medical" Life

In my early years of college and seminary, in order to pay bills, I had the experience of working in hospitals. I was soon "promoted" from orderly to being trusted to work in the operating and recovery rooms, as well as in emergency on the weekends. For a short time while at college, I worked as a surgical technician in a Chicago hospital. The variety of experiences afforded to me, as one with no formal medical training, was unique and, I believe, God directed. It exposed me to a vast set of human relationships and cultural differences that affected my view of life significantly.

Firefighter

In my first pastorate in the United States near Wheaton, Illinois, I became a volunteer firefighter. That was indeed a colorful time as I learned how to drive and operate a huge fire rig as part of a three-vehicle contingent that would go rushing out of the village where we lived, heading to fires in local factories, farms, or isolated residences in the countryside. It involved water rescue from drowning or vehicle crashes. We met regularly for drills and training. I became close to those colleagues.

Both these categories of endeavor not only gave me exposure to cultural variety but also gave me great stories to tell my grandchildren about firefighting rescue escapades and medical emergencies, such as assisting in delivering a baby in the back of a Volkswagen on a snowy night when the car couldn't make the hill to the hospital.

"Join Something"

Often in discussion I am asked how one can get engaged effectively in the culture in which we live. My list above in this chapter can be added to by thousands of people who joined choirs, orchestras, clubs, sports, bands, book clubs, and a myriad of other such things (some of which I note in the epilogue to this book when suggesting ways in which we can "live compassionately"). We all have different interests, skills, and passions, therefore we all have opportunity to "join something" and thus get involved in the lives of others.

A Celtic Story

Throughout this book I mention my interest in the story of the Celts, from their early beginning in their pre-Christian days in Europe through to the conversion of Ireland via St. Patrick and the influence of the so-named Celtic church that lasted until about the ninth century. Today *Celtic* can mean a host of things, such as Celtic jewelry, Celtic music, Celtic mysticism, and so on. A brief but helpful book, *Rediscovering the Celts: The True Witness from Western Shores*, was written by Martin Robinson, the former director of the British Bible Society.[2]

One day I was having tea in a shop in the lovely village of Fort Langley, British Columbia, when I noticed an advertisement for those who would be interested in a series of "Celtic discussions." I followed the ad and showed up one Friday night to a collection of very diverse people who wanted to be part of these Friday evenings. Every worldview seemed to be in attendance, with practitioners of New Ageism, Buddhist meditation, yoga, existentialism, Indigenous spirituality, Witchcraft, so-called Celtic spirituality, and much more.

Every Friday involved different presentations that were varied and discussions that were robust. We learned about Buddhist meditation, Indigenous sweat lodges, and Celtic life (the secular versions). One evening the leader proposed that we do role-plays from Dungeons and Dragons. I gulped and tensed up, but before I could say anything, a Jewish lady addressed the group and said that she must not participate because as a Jew she saw that as witchcraft, and that was forbidden by her Judaism. The leader of our evening said that we would cancel that out of respect to her.

---

2. Robinson, *Rediscovering the Celts*.

A Tale of Two Cultures

This was the nature and spirit of the group. I was asked one Friday evening to share what I knew about the Christian era of the Celts.

A few weeks later it was Good Friday, and I had the choice, in my mind at least, of going to a Good Friday service or attending my regular Friday evening with my "Celtic" group; I chose the latter. When I got there, the leader stated that he hadn't really prepared a topic, but as it was Good Friday for Christians, he asked if would I present what Good Friday and Easter weekend was all about. I did just that and led discussions afterwards. By belonging to a world outside of my Christian world, I had once more experienced two cultures as I sought to seek first the kingdom of God and his righteousness.

When I was in my senior year at Wheaton College, I had lunch with a campus guest. She was a very competent Jewish lady in her early thirties. Her role was to come on campus and share with students of Jewish background the value of living in Israel after graduation. I spoke to a somewhat discouraged young woman because the response to her by Jewish students across the United States had not been encouraging. Her word to me was that she understood in a new way the biblical phrase that not all who claimed to be Israel were Israel. There is a similar challenge to Christians. We live in two worlds at the same time, which we can name as the kingdom of God and the secular kingdom. The Bible teaches that although we are in the world, our goals, values, mission, lifestyle, and ethos come from God's design for life in his kingdom.[3]

Values

Wherever my wife, Brenda, and I raised our three children, whatever churches we served as they were growing up, the lens through which we taught them to see life was the kingdom of God. We tried to model to them Matt 6:33: seek first God's kingdom. That goal contained many values. One which we taught them was stewardship. In the 1980s, I left Canada to serve in England. One summer during that period, I traveled back from England to North America to continue in doctoral studies. Before returning to my church in England, I visited Cameron, my son, at Wheaton College. He told me he had concerns about his tithe. His concern was not regarding whether to pay his tithe out of his wages from his part-time job. His concern was that his job at a mental health clinic prevented him from attending one

---

3. John 17:6–19; Rom 12:1–3; 2 Cor 10:1–5.

specific church on Sundays in the summer until he returned to college. He wanted to know where he should give his tithe. That thinking was the result of a kingdom value with which he had grown up. The selflessness of faithful stewardship remains with all my children to this day.

Cameron was just a babe in arms when one wintry evening after church, Brenda slipped on the icy steps of the church building and hurt herself badly. Cameron was unhurt. After medical treatment, days later we were contacted by the insurance company concerning medical compensation. The problem was that they wanted us to sue the church for us to have a case. We refused, believing that such an action to fellow believers was not the life of the kingdom. Fortunately, after much discussion, they relented. If they hadn't, we would not have been compensated.

I loved to wear real leather shoes for dress-up occasions. One day, I chanced upon a big sale at a department store, and to my surprise, I found a top-of-the-line pair of shoes in a section marked at twenty dollars. I could hardly believe my eyes. I looked carefully at the sticker. It stated twenty dollars. I was not at peace. These were surely two-hundred-and-fifty-dollar shoes (as this was twenty-five years ago, they might have been equivalent to four hundred dollars today). I took the shoes and passed by other sections. There in a more exclusive stall was the same pair that I had taken. They were indeed listed at two hundred and fifty dollars. I went to the cashier and asked to speak to the manager. I explained to her my situation. She took my shoes and said she would check things out. She returned and said the shoes I had chosen were indeed two hundred and fifty dollars and that they had been mismarked and put in the wrong section. Then she added that I was the first person in her twenty years at the store who had come to her as I had. She told me to take the shoes and told the cashier to charge me twenty dollars. I still have those shoes today. I don't wear them often anymore, but whenever I do, I am reminded that in all things I am to seek the kingdom of God and his righteousness.

Let me stress that these simple everyday anecdotes that I make about values can pale in light of greater issues that we can face when, in response to life's situations, we seek first the kingdom of God. Some people lose their employment because they will not compromise their Christian values and principles. Others become impoverished because they applied the principles that Jesus taught.[4] Still others can miss out on political position because they oppose populist theories.

---

4. "Watch out! Be on your guard against all kinds of greed; life does not consist in an

A Tale of Two Cultures

The beautiful story of Ruth and Boaz, in the book of Ruth, is a gentle example of lives lived with integrity, honesty, and trust, all of which are part of kingdom thinking and behavior. Dallas Willard portrays this mindset in his book *The Allure of Gentleness*.[5] This is the foundation for making the most compelling argument for Christianity, one that will convince others that there is something special about Christianity and the kingdom of Jesus, which is a priority in our lives.

INSIGHTS

The Cultural Journey

There are almost as many books on Christians and culture as there are books about God's kingdom. I insert this reminder that I am not presenting an academic or scholarly approach to the many intricacies and problems about understanding culture. I am writing that it is important that we understand that we as believers are meant to be operating out of different narratives of life and with a different mindset.

Seeking the kingdom and desiring to live righteously as part of the Christian life needs to be front and center in our dialogue with our culture, but we cannot do that unless we are lovingly and deeply involved in it. My anecdotes above only represent how I dealt with the issue; there are many different approaches, given all our unique circumstances. But by seeking first God's kingdom, we have the best hope of not being so controlled by the culture.

Following God and doing his will is certainly no longer an important value in an age of individualism. Everything is a personal choice. For example, people often say something like, "I am spiritual but not religious." This mindset of doing one's own thing, what is best for oneself, is now deeply imbedded in the culture. Many church members, while they "do church" faithfully and sincerely, may not know the real heart of what the gospel was intended to be. Many Christians struggle with the fact that their cultural habits/values generally do not equate with what life in the

---

abundance of possessions" (Luke 12:15).

5. Dallas Willard, in his book *The Allure of Gentleness*, expresses a similar theme that we must be transformed people living out a life reflective of Jesus himself; a life of love, humility, and gentleness.

kingdom of God was meant to be (and particularly what it will need to be in these coming turbulent years).

In Jer 29, the Jews lived out the kingdom of Jehovah in a foreign land. The book of Daniel is about God's people living in a world that was so totally different to what they had been accustomed and taught from their childhood. Daniel shows us how to live a life of spiritual integrity in the crush of a secular world. Both Daniel and Jesus knew that they were part of a different kingdom, just as we believers are today. We live in a society of shallow axioms and assumptions that shape our lives. We will need to teach ourselves to think spiritually and biblically about life's issues. We do not know God's ways just because we sense something or because it feels right. We know his ways because God has revealed them to us in the Bible, and we have experienced the consensus of spiritually minded believers throughout the ages. Interpreting Scripture in light of our contemporary culture is a challenging task, but the more vital task is to interpret and understand the culture in light of Scripture, especially in a world of changing social mores. This kind of exegesis will show us that our life in the kingdom is about pleasing God, not about pleasing ourselves or choosing self-actualization; it is more about choosing self-denial.

David Fitch has written extensively about how we deal with culture as believers. In his book, *The Great Giveaway*, he states that the church has given away so much of its biblical mandate that it is left with nothing much to do but to deliver goods, services, and information to individuals.[6] It is, as a result, left to be a sideshow while most Christians live by the edicts, values, and ethos of the culture in which they find themselves. Because of our emphasis on individuals rather than community, we borrow concepts from the world to meet the felt needs of those individuals. According to Fitch, the choice for the church in every age will always be to ask whether our identity and lifestyle will primarily be shaped by Scripture or by our culture—by the biblical story or the cultural story. He elaborates on these views in two of his other books: *Faithful Presence* and *The Church of Us vs. Them*, in which he stresses that we neither judge nor accommodate to the culture but live as good news among our neighbors.[7]

---

6. Fitch, *Great Giveaway*, 13.
7. Fitch, *Faithful Presence*, 26; Fitch, *Church of Us*, 25.

A Tale of Two Cultures

A Cosmic Battle

I find it difficult to believe in the devil and try not to think about it often, but I cannot hide behind my position. I believe in Jesus, and he believed in Satan and his evil forces in the world and the inevitable clash of two kingdoms. I watch the world in which we live, and I observe through novels, movies, videos, music, and such that so many in our present culture do believe in Satan and evil forces, often more than Christians do.

Satanic forces battle against the kingdom of God. Satan holds a kingdom as well. Jesus battled Satan in the wilderness.[8] If we are to live for the kingdom of God and give its lifestyle preeminence in our lives, then we need to be aware of the battle that believers face. This aspect of our cultural struggle with the world in which we live as believers needs a thorough deliberation, which I have chosen not to take on in this book. I believe however that the subject is important, and so I recommend Oxford scholar Michael Green's book, *I Believe in Satan's Downfall: The Reality of Evil and the Victory of Christ*.

The Down-to-Earth Struggle

Contemporary cultural influences present us with individualism, narcissism, anti-authority, and anti-truth, as well as inadequate definitions of the good life where everything must yield to satisfaction and happiness. The result is amnesia about everything except the immediate, the instant, the now, and the me. To seek first the kingdom in this setting is difficult. The vision of the kingdom and the direction of the culture we live in present a different outlook, as it was for Daniel and his three friends, Shadrach, Meshach, and Abednego. They were part of a different mindset than Babylon, but God instructed them to be an integral part of their exilic culture. Daniel's story is one of extraordinary faith in God lived out in the full glare of national and local life that became increasingly antagonistic to his faith. Today, this is just as challenging for believers as it was for Daniel in Babylon. He served the kingdom well, and so can we.

---

8. Ephesians 2:2 calls Satan "the ruler of the kingdom of the air." We are reminded of this fact in Luke 4:1–13 when Jesus spent forty days in the wilderness where he was tempted by the devil. We read in verses 5–7 that Satan "showed him in an instant all the kingdoms of the world. And he said to him, 'I will give you all their authority and splendor; it has been given to me, and I can give it to anyone I want to. If you worship me, it will all be yours.'"

Staying Clearheaded

The wonderful teachings of Paul about his own cultural shifts as a Christian, which he notes in Phil 3, arise out of the fact that after his conversion in Acts 9, he went away for three years (Gal 1:13–24) to be shown a new cultural life with new identity, new purposes, and new goals (Phil 3:14).

If we want to communicate the gospel to a different culture, we need to speak in the language of the culture to which we are communicating. While all this is true and helpful, it is important for Christians to realize also that what Daniel and his friends offered was a willingness to serve the Babylonian culture well, while at the same time being resolved to stand up to it, as the fiery furnace in Dan 3 and the lion's den in Dan 6 clearly reveal. Daniel and his friends knew how to seek first the kingdom while deeply imbedded in a foreign culture.

The church only hurts itself by trying to be acceptable and relevant for the sake of it. There is great danger in congregations letting secular cultural values shape theological convictions in order to show care for those struggling with biblical values. We must not package Christianity in a way that the church is barely distinguishable from other social agencies and altruistic enterprises in our society; this Daniel refused to do. We face this in matters such as gender orientation, abortion, divorce, political power, climate change, and a host of other issues. The temptation to conform can be very subtle; rationalizations come easily. Culture shapes, controls, and determines our thinking far more than we realize. I think that this is, in part at least, what Matt 6:33 is implying. The tension will always be how we hold conviction and compassion at the same time, but we must keep in mind that there are challenges and costs to being a citizen of God's kingdom. As Daniel and his three friends, we are to live as a distinct minority who care for and are involved in the very culture that marginalizes us.

Having read John McKnight, I have come to realize that our neighbors don't see us as citizens of another kingdom when they see us consumed by malls, money, cars, clothes, vacations, and houses—as we tend to be.[9] The church has been shaped for so long by a Christian culture that has been sold out to modernity and all that it entails. The kingdom of God is meant to be the lens through which Christians are to see the world. Matthew 6:33 gives us belonging and purpose; it gives us our sense of identity as Christians.

---

9. McKnight and Block, *Abundant Community*.

A Tale of Two Cultures

Ambivalence

We are part of the culture in which we live, and we must deal with that in love and compassion. We will need to live in these difficult days with some sense of ambivalence; in other words, on many cultural things there are not one-line answers or solutions. We share life in society with others whom God loves but who don't share many of our Christian values. As I note above, we will always have to face our own inner tension between compassion for others and our valid convictions derived from Scripture. While the secular culture often stands in contrast to kingdom culture, and Christians are tempted to capitulate to it, we must not live out our values with a "them versus us" mentality.

As I wrote at the start of this chapter, it was perhaps my Liverpool environment that gave to me the sense of ambivalence (i.e., the ability to see things from both sides and not be thrown by things that were plainly countercultural to me). The ambivalence is that of being with neighbors and club members and work associates and yet knowing of a different world than theirs without typecasting, condemning, or judging them. Regardless of how we were raised, we are confronted in our modern culture with a lifestyle radically different from what is taught in the Bible. We must make difficult decisions. We make them best when we understand that Daniel and his three friends in Dan 1 had more than head knowledge about Jehovah; their identity came out of their devotion to him.

Lesslie Newbigin in his *Foolishness to the Greeks: The Gospel and Western Culture* expresses his concerns about gospel and culture. Throughout the book he reiterates that there must be both solidarity with our culture as well as separation from its idolatry.[10]

POINTS TO PONDER

If the Scriptures may be trusted, then life is about pleasing God, not about pleasing ourselves. We are called to speak out of a different cultural narrative than the secular world; one that is guided by Matt 6:33.

---

10. Newbigin, *Foolishness to the Greeks*.

Two Worlds

As children grow up, they are shaped by parental values that, however kind and loving they might have been, may not have seen life through the lens of God's kingdom. As children become teens, they may submit to peer pressure that often lacks much that is godly. By the time that they become adults, they adopt, almost by osmosis, a way of life that looks like the culture around them. That "secular" mindset shapes their decisions and plans—unless they discover the dynamic of belonging to another kingdom.

For younger believers the changes happening in all of society that seem frightening to an older generation are less dramatic because basically what is now before them is all they have ever known of cultural values, which for the most part have long drifted from the kingdom of God. Most young people have never known anything other than the chaotic, internet-defined reality of the twenty-first century in which peer culture shapes, controls, and determines far more than ever before. Parents, politicians, and pastors are running to keep up. We must not resent this and be critical but rather seek ways to help. I know the difficulty of repeating in today's culture any approach to learning from a past era (even a Christian lifestyle), particularly to a second generation or split-parent family.

There is a helpful biblical principle to be found in Deut 6:6–9: "These commandments that I give you today are to be on your hearts. Impress them on your children. Talk about them when you sit at home and when you walk along the road, when you lie down and when you get up. Tie them as symbols on your hands and bind them on your foreheads. Write them on the doorframes of your houses and on your gates."

What we can do for our children is to equip them to live in society (culture) fearlessly, confidently, and productively. However, this may not necessarily be achieved by sending them to Christian institutions, or even by hyperchurch activity, but rather by the modeling influence of the home environment with its values and vision of life lived for God. I want to make this sensitive caveat; namely that however faithfully and skillfully parents model Matt 6:33, we must realize that children grow up to be individuals who chart their own destiny by their own choices. The cultural pressures on them are enormous, through school for one example. I have known very dedicated parents who sought *to seek first the kingdom* and raised their children with care and love only to find that one or more of their offspring did not imbibe or accept either their convictions or their values. It is a mystery buried deep in the reality of human autonomy. Notwithstanding this, plus the very different models and configurations of "family" that exist today, the recovery of family education remains vital for Christians in this culture. Hugh Halter, in his book *Righteous Brood: Making the Mission of God a Family Story*, gives excellent guidance in this whole area.

Christian communities will need to help single-parent families and those families who can rarely be together due to the economic pressures that scatter them each day to such different work schedules. Even if in all we do, we truly seek first the kingdom of God and his righteousness while immersed in and committed to the society in which we live, we may not always get the cultural issues right. But we will be more fulfilled and effective in our Christian walk.

APPENDIX

Books

- Tim Keller's *Center Church* incorporates Richard Niebuhr's framework from *Christ and Culture* into a simpler perspective
- In his book *Culture Making*, Andy Crouch writes that it is not enough to condemn culture or critique culture or copy or consume culture but to offer an alternative transforming culture via the kingdom of God
- Lesslie Newbigin's *The Gospel in a Pluralistic Society*, *The Open Secret*, and *Foolishness to the Greeks* are probably the most pertinent of Newbigin's contributions to church and culture
- David E. Fitch, *Faithful Presence: Seven Disciplines That Shape the Church for Mission*
- Mark Sayers, *Disappearing Church: From Cultural Relevance to Gospel Resilience*

CHAPTER 4

Community and Mission

The longing for community is deep within most, but so few ever experience it well.

—Parker Palmer[1]

To seek first the kingdom of God and his righteousness is not meant to be a lonely or individualistic journey. By design, in both Scripture and nature, we are meant to be part of a collective life, in a similar manner to how we mature as children in the context of family.

In this chapter, I want to share stories that may help us to understand elements of *life together*. I have struggled long and hard to grasp what meaningful Christian community is all about. These stories that follow are, in essence, like a kaleidoscope as I go from the general (a variety of groupings in society that I observed as one-off events, which can be a taste of the community that is so wonderfully portrayed in the book of Acts) to the specific (possible characteristics of a functioning Christian community).

Community is a fluid and existential thing. Like love, it is a more observable than definable experience. Life together is more caught than taught, programmed, or planned, but I hope to point to ways in which expressions of life together can effectively be made by God's people in today's world. It seems to be God's plan to have believers function as an alternative model to our struggling culture.

---

1. Palmer, *Place Called Community*, 4.

STORIES

Flash Mob

Barcelona continues to be my favorite city. While I was a church leader in England, I went to Barcelona as often as I could. About twenty kilometers north of Barcelona, still in Catalonia, is the small textile town of Sabadell. It was there about ten years ago in a typical flash-mob encounter that I was able, through YouTube, to watch a single cellist begin playing in the market square the melody "Ode to Joy" from Beethoven's Ninth Symphony.[2] Slowly he was joined by other musicians who took up the theme he was playing. People entering the square became interested. More musicians and then singers kept arriving, as well as a real orchestra conductor. To some degree it must have been planned, but there was also a lot of spontaneity as children started mimicking their efforts with great joy, climbed lampposts to get a better view, or danced with excitement with their parents' approval. Every generation entered the town square to listen, and as the crowds grew, people began singing the words of "Ode to Joy" as if they were a mass choir. I was amazed that so many knew the words, but perhaps I shouldn't have been because the original words about brotherhood/sisterhood are part of a quasi-European national anthem.

The coming together of the "Ode to Joy" crowd was born in part because of the sense of community that seems common in small European towns with a town square, where people often meet to celebrate festive holidays. How much was *community* in the flash mob event and how much was simply *communalism* is hard to define, but what I saw that day was togetherness, spontaneity, openness, a sense of belonging and joy of the human spirit, as well as cooperative effort and appreciation of one another.

Although I am not sure how to label what I experienced watching the actions of the townsfolk in this Sabadell square, it was quite an event that for me carried the exuberance needed in church gatherings. The sense of *togetherness, community,* and *belonging* were so evident in the market square event that afternoon. I was touched. This was a place in which people bonded in a common enterprise, and in which I felt hope.

---

2. Banco Sabadell, "Som Sabadell Flashmob."

"Village" Pubs

Many older North Americans who enjoyed *Cheers*, the TV sitcom about life in a Boston bar in the 1980s to 1990s, will be able to identify with my next story, as it includes some of my observations and identifications about an English "village" pub during the same period of time. I put the word "village" in quotations because such a setting can be both rural or urban. Wherever pubs exist they tend to be places of togetherness and camaraderie.

I moved my family back to Britain in the 1980s, and we lived in Guildford, England, some thirty-five kilometers from London, an idyllic historic town surrounded by rural villages with quaint names such as Gomshall, Abinger Hammer, Peaslake, and Shere. I would often walk my Springer Spaniel, Jenny, from my Guildford house and head across wooded vales and country lanes to the village of Shere, which was steeped in medieval history and Tudor buildings. It has been listed as one of the most beautiful villages in England. Not far away was the little town of Dorking. Its claim to fame is a pub where many of those who sailed on the Mayflower to America met to plan their trip. The village pub in Shere is named the White Horse. It was a meeting place for friends to gather and chat away many hours. Whenever I visited the pub, I was urged not leave my dog outside but to bring her in by the fireside. (She was well pleased.) The pub was not just a place to eat and drink but to share and enjoy one another's presence and to continue relationships week after week. This all would intensify at Christmastime, when the most popular thing on the menu would be a rack of lamb. My family would book a table weeks ahead, and when we arrived, we would sit at the window near a roaring fire to have dinner. That scene into which we entered had been repeated since about the fifteenth century. As we ate, the church choir from St. James parish (whose first vicar served in AD 1207) showed up in the courtyard outside the window singing carols. This was all so wonderful, but I realize that it doesn't define community as such but shows our human desire to enjoy life together.

Coffee Shops

I couldn't walk from my house in Guildford to a Parisian coffee shop, but somewhat regularly I would take a quick train trip by Eurotunnel to Paris, arrive at Gare du Nord in about three hours, and sit at a coffee shop to enjoy similar experiences to those of Shere and *Cheers*. Eventually, I would make my way from Gare du Nord to a "village" situated on the top of the funicular that lifted one to the Sacred Heart Basilica. Montmartre is a wonderful experience of community in the dozens of coffee shops and cafés that exist up there. People gather to wine and dine away the hours. To complete my little jaunts to Paris, I would also go from Gare du Nord to walk down through "urban villages" composed mostly of African immigrants with all their remarkable features and cafés and creative community life. Eventually, I would arrive at Notre Dame Cathedral and the nearby Latin Quarter, full of coffee shops where writers, artists, and philosophers of renown have spent hours visiting and exchanging their outlook. This was all part of some form of community.

There are of course such experiences in coffee shops and cafés throughout North America and the rest of the world. I remember fondly my motorbike trips to Lynden, Washington, just down the road from Langley, British Columbia, where I lived. I visited one or two cafés, but one in particular seemed to be full of a group of older men who met there two or three times a week for breakfast. They knew and cared for one another. That was also a form of community.

While we are looking at pubs, cafés, and the like as places of community, this vignette from David Fitch's book, *Faithful Presence*, takes place at McDonald's of all places:

> Several years ago, I started going to a McDonald's in my neighborhood. There, early in the morning, I would drink coffee, grade papers, do research, have meetings, and do other things pastors and professors do. A friend eventually challenged me to see this local McDonald's as the arena of God's Spirit at work. Instead of seeing it as merely a place to do my own work, instead of even seeing the hundreds of people that pass by as candidates for my "come to Jesus" evangelism speech, I was challenged to see this place as a vibrant arena where God was truly present. I was exhorted to enter this place peacefully and be present with every person who came my way, pay attention to all that was going around me, and tend to God's presence here. For a few hours in the early morning, I started to do that regularly. As time went on I started to meet an array of people in surprising conversations. I got to know people struggling to hold onto a job, abused by a spouse, or mistreated by police. I got to know some police themselves. I shared tables regularly with people who lived in cars and vans. I became enmeshed in a network where God was working in people's lives, and I was swept up into it. I had never been invited into the lives of so

many people as I was at this McDonald's (not even in a church). We encountered God together. I saw miracles of God's presence materialize before my very eyes (some of which I'll tell about in this book). I found myself joined with people in prayer.[3]

San Paulo and Other Places

I experienced life together for a few weeks in San Paulo, Brazil, in a favela among very poor Christians who were surrounded by drug lords and other suppressive people. Despite all the deprivations they experienced, they loved Jesus and indeed understood Matt 6:33. I attended a party where the birthday cake was dried white bread soaked in sugar, with a candle stuck in it. I saw people care for and support one other in remarkable ways and live out their life together in worship and discipleship in the most ghastly of circumstances.

My experience of the motorcycle club to which I belonged was certainly a form of community. There are intentional societies that form life together and function around common goals and causes and so, in a sense, are labeled as communities. There are cohousing communes; a society named Windsong existed in my own neighborhood in Langley and near Vancouver (residents owned their own homes but shared several group facilities, activities, and responsibilities together each day). Many communities carry the idea of commitment to shared life principles and have some rules or even some form of a covenant. I faithfully followed the Hallmark TV series *When Calls the Heart*, which is about community life in a small Canadian mining town at the beginning of the twentieth century. *Anne of Green Gables* is a similar story of community life in Prince Edward Island during the same period. Andre Rieu, the Dutch violinist and music entrepreneur, formed the Strauss Orchestra that has made so many tours of the world presenting concerts. The bond between all the members of the company formed by Rieu so obviously has the marks of true community.

Indigenous and Challenged Groups

In North America and Australia, indigenous nations live out community in so many ways and have so much to teach us about corporate life together. Henri Nouwen, about whom I will relate in chapter 6, was a well-known

3. Fitch, *Faithful Presence*, 11.

Catholic scholar and Christian writer. He lived with the Daybreak L'Arche community in Toronto for several years until his death in 1996. Founded in 1964 by Jean Vanier, Raphaël Simi, and Philip Seux, L'Arche emerged as a reaction and a community-based alternative to the ill-treatment and dismal living conditions in the psychiatric institutions of the 1960s. The goal was to build a world where people with and without intellectual disabilities are friends and equals. L'Arche consists of nearly one hundred and sixty communities, present in thirty-seven countries in extremely diversified cultural, religious, and socioeconomic contexts. Those communities are places where the mission is to help society gain from the rich talents, insights, and experiences of people with intellectual disabilities. The L'Arche Charter says, "In a divided world, L'Arche wants to be a sign of hope. Its communities, founded on covenant relationships between people of differing intellectual capacity, social origin, religion and culture, seek to be signs of unity, faithfulness and reconciliation."[4]

In my hometown of Kelowna, there is a similar sense of community in a building created by Hadgraft and Wilson that includes a community of challenged people. While it was not formally structured as L'Arche is, the life of a caring community is evident. Recently, the building became unsafe because of an adjacent massive building project's excavation. Meeting very soon after the evacuation notice, there was no attempt to lay blame or talk of legal action but only to share loving, simple talk of care for each other and trust that God would provide. These beautiful people exhibited the true spirit of a loving community. They understood Matt 5:5: "Blessed are the meek, for they will inherit the earth."

INSIGHTS

Heinz Soup

Heinz soup once advertised that it had fifty-seven varieties to taste. There may be a variety of experiences concerning what *community* could mean and how it expresses itself in everyday life. There is no one model or definition of life together. The books which are written about different concepts and expressions of community would fill huge sections of any well-stocked library. Sociologists and social philosophers have theories, principles,

---

4. L'Arche International, *Charter*, 4.

characteristics, and models about community.[5] Their contributions seem to offer neat and clean definitions, but I do not think that these categories or divisions are that simple, which is part of the reason for my stories.

Robert Banks, in his classic *Paul's Idea of Community*, comments on passages that show how the early church behaved, and he wonders if these Scriptures are only expressions of their beginning life together rather than rigid principles about community set in stone forever.[6] The point here is that we are given insights into their life together that can encourage and guide us about how to live as a fellowship of the Holy Spirit today. We are not given an inflexible how-to manual or formula. Effective community is mostly born of openness, among a bonding few, to what the Spirit is calling them to do. Community can't be manufactured by human programming; it grows out of an understanding and desire related to Matt 6:33 and a commitment to each other. It is the response of some to the call of God and influence of the Spirit upon their lives. Within this context, their relationships are voluntarily open to accountability and to care for each other. Being a community and a people is a gift from God. For years, I wrote manuals on cell groups as a basis for church community life. I lectured on them and organized a system of how they were supposed to work. I still cherish the models of community that I have experienced through the years, and I know of numerous churches effectively having cell/mission groups or some form of small groups in order to bring members closer to responsibility, accountability, and meaningful relationships with each other and with their neighborhoods.

My understanding is that the early church, just after Pentecost, believed that fellowship, discipleship, caring for others, worship, and mission were part of their new community life together (Acts 2). They didn't form a committee or hold seminars to create mission statements about their common life. What happened was primarily the work of the Spirit in the newly born

---

5. In his book *Different Drum: Community Making and Peace*, Scott Peck says that community has three essential ingredients: inclusivity, commitment, and consensus. Author A. J. Swoboda highlights that Zygmunt Bauman has suggested two kinds of community. He calls them *peg communities* and *ethical communities*. Peg communities are forged by disconnected spectators around a mutual experience, such as a hockey game. They are involved in a common experience but have little attachment to one another. Swoboda goes on to state that "ethical communities, in stark contrast, are long-term commitments that are marked by the giving up of rights and of service. In short, ethical communities are built on relationships of responsibilities to one another." Swoboda, *Subversive Sabbath*, 68.

6. Banks, *Paul's Idea of Community*.

lives of those first converts. Dietrich Bonhoeffer, in his book *Life Together*, saw Christian community as a gift of God; it is a reality created by God.[7]

Social media has added another dimension to human social connectedness. While it offers a level of community online, to succeed it will have to put down roots in the offline world. Physical communities have a depth that virtual communities can't achieve. Parker Palmer in one of his early books, *A Place Called Community*, stresses that to live in a community is to be visible and accountable. Community is important to God and to God's people. Growth occurs best in a caring community. There are spiritual truths we will never grasp and Christian standards we will never attain except as we share in community with other believers. The Holy Spirit ministers to us, in large measure, through each other.[8]

Church of the Saviour, Washington, DC

A long time ago I was given funds by a benefactor that enabled me to pay for an itinerary to visit leaders in North America who, I believed, understood my own quest for community. One of those leaders was Elizabeth O'Connor, who worked with Gordon Cosby at the Church of the Saviour. Her book, *Call to Commitment*, tells the story of the church and its deep sense of a committed life together.[9] When I landed at the Washington, DC, airport, I hired a taxi and asked the driver to take me to the Church of the Saviour on 2020 Massachusetts Ave. He said there was no church on that street. I said that there was, and so we bantered back and forth until we arrived at the place. We were both right. In the normal sense, there was no church edifice, no stained-glass windows or steeple, just a large, old mansion. At the top of the steps at the front door on a shiny brass plate was the sign: Headquarters Where the Church of the Saviour Sometimes Meets. This epitomized the life and message of this remarkable church. The days I spent there, I was guided by Elizabeth O'Connor, who showed me a people living out Acts 2 and 4. I was particularly moved when she took me to Potter's House, the coffee shop / restaurant where many of the leaders in the US House and Senate would drop in and engage in dialogue. The network of small groups to which people covenanted to belong and serve each year

---

7. Bonhoeffer, *Life Together*, 25.

8. This is what Paul is talking about in Eph 4:15–16 and to the contemporary population longing for authenticity.

9. O'Connor, *Call to Commitment*.

was the basis of a membership striving for true community. The *Handbook for Mission Groups* by Gordon Cosby was a manual laying out the principles for forming small intentional groups of Christian believers, with a focus on developing both personal gifts and the gifts of others in ministering to each other and the surrounding world.[10]

Spirit Not Sentiment

In many churches, the focus is the clergyperson, the church building, the Sunday service, or a church board. This is not how it is meant to be because the church, more than any other major institution in our society, contains the potential for true community life. In seeking community, we need to avoid the danger of romanticism and sentimentalism about the quest for our life together. Community is more dynamic than a nostalgia for good times of fellowship. On the opposite end of the emotional spectrum, while it is not about "warm fuzzies," it is also not about some pragmatic approach to structuring church life. The dream of life together, however sincere, can carry romantic notions wherein people spend their time and effort with each other for the sake of mutual relationships.[11] Community is not about warm relationships per se but about learning and growing together, about discoveries and change in the context of mission.[12] True and effective community is not handed to us on a plate. It comes as a result of slow growth and maturity in both our relationship to others and through our spiritual journey and relationship with God.

The work of an effective life-together group is long and often hard, like the pilgrimage on the Camino de Santiago. The movie *The Way* portrays the spiritual journey of a father who lost his son on a religious pilgrimage in Europe and stars Martin Sheen. After losing his son, Daniel, in France, Tom, an American eye doctor, decides to walk the same path that took his son's life. Returning to France to pick up Daniel's body, Tom learns all about the path his son was taking, the Camino de Santiago. He spreads his son's

---

10. Cosby, *Handbook for Mission Groups*.

11. Dietrich Bonhoeffer wrote, "He who loves his dream of community rather than the community itself will ultimately destroy the community." *Life Together*, 11.

12. "The very purpose of [Christ's] self-giving on the cross was not just to save isolated individuals, and so perpetrate their loneliness, but to create a new community whose members would belong to him, love one another, and eagerly serve the world." Stott, *Cross of Christ*, 255.

ashes along the pilgrim's path his son had walked. Staying in hostels along the way, Tom meets a robust Dutchman, Joost, a chain-smoking Canadian, Sarah, and Jack, an Irish writer. Each of these people are walking the path for different reasons. They form a community of sorts, out of a common goal.[13] Wikipedia reports that since 2013, the Camino de Santiago has attracted more than two hundred thousand pilgrims each year.[14] Pilgrims come mainly on foot, requiring days or weeks of walking to reach Santiago. For many the journey is transformative, as the life of true community is meant to be.

In the Christian world, in many denominations, there are monasteries and convents, which are spiritual communities. Hutterites, Amish, and Doukhobors are ethnic Christian communities in Canada, while Taizé in France and Iona, Lindisfarne, and Nether Springs in the UK are further contemporary models of Christian life together. In history, there have been numerous attempts at utopian communal life, such as Herrnhut led by Count Zinzendorf, who was such an influence on John Wesley in the eighteenth century. In New York, the Chautauqua Institution was founded in 1874 by inventor Lewis Miller and Methodist Bishop John Heyl Vincent as a teaching camp for Sunday school teachers. In the one hundred and fifty years since its inception, it has become a high-quality community learning the arts, religion, politics, and seeking peace.

For most of my ministry in the various places where I have lived, I have retreated each week or fortnight to such settings. When I lived in Calgary, I went almost every Tuesday to the Mount Francis Retreat Centre in Cochrane (not far from Banff) for a day of prayer, reflection, and study. When it was supper time, I was able to join the friars for both a meal and an evening of sharing with them. There I began my journey into appreciating Francis of Assisi and his close friend Clare, who founded the Order of Poor Ladies (Poor Clares). These two saints formed Christian communities in Assisi at San Damiano in the thirteenth century. I visited Assisi twice, once as a tourist and once as a pilgrim, where I experienced the power of life together in a new way, as I soaked myself in the remarkable story of Francis and Clare in the very place where they lived. I sat with tears in Clare's prayer room at San Damiano, overcome by the realization of the community life they had known there. When living in other cities, I was privileged to be a guest for a day at various convents; these were deep communities indeed.

13. Estevez, *Way*.
14. Wikipedia, "Camino de Santiago."

Kingdom First

In many cities around the world today, there are Christian communities dedicated to caring for the poor and needy. They are far too numerous to list, but one is The Simple Way in Philadelphia, founded by Shane Claiborne. Many other similar communities can be formed of both local residents in a given neighborhood and members scattered worldwide, in extension of the ideals and goals of any given community.

I recall some years ago spending a week at the Church of the Redeemer (Anglican/Episcopal) in Houston, Texas. It had undergone a remarkable experience of renewal under Graham Pulkingham. By the time I visited the church, the new leader (vicar) was Jeff Shiftmeir. The story of the church's transformation is quite remarkable and was featured in *Time* magazine, on national TV networks, and in a book written by Michael Harper, *A New Way of Living*.[15] In a nutshell, the story is that of a church in an old and declining neighborhood with social chaos, crime, poverty, and very needy immigrant people. The church itself was struggling to survive. The school was a scary place, and social needs were not being met. Most of the congregation lived in the more affluent suburbs and traveled in to attend church. When the renewal came, things changed swiftly, and many of them left their comfortable housing and vocations to move into the neighborhood around the church building. Some took up communal living in local houses. The school became serviced by Christian teachers who resigned their positions in the more affluent Houston suburbs, sold up, and moved into the area around the Church of the Redeemer. Other professionals (doctors, lawyers, etc.) did the same thing in their field. Such transformations took place everywhere. The school solved the drug and dropout issues, the neighborhood had a new lease on life, while the church became a place to belong—not just to visit on Sunday. They served the neighbors with all kinds of care, such as purchasing food from local farms and selling them at low prices to the residents around the church. As in Acts 4, they indeed won the favor of all the people. My week with them was one of the most uplifting of my life. On Wednesday evening during my visit, I heard the church bell ring at about five o'clock in the evening, summoning everyone who wanted to attend supper at the church, and was touched to see doors open in houses around the neighborhood and people walking with each other to the church building where not only did they eat a meal but also shared clothing and goods as needed, as well as practise together for the songs and ministries that would happen on Sunday. There

---

15. Harper, *New Way of Living*, 40–42.

was much more during the week, but their story can be seen on YouTube or by reading Michael Harper's book.[16] The whole experience confirmed to me that mission is a vital expression of life together; the Church of the Redeemer had both.

POINTS TO PONDER

Community needs to be born out of a heart's desire. It is lived with various people in various ways. Our life together is the fruit of people living authentically and lovingly with an expanding pool of growing friendships that defies age, interests, ethnicity, and societal status. It involves accountability, responsibility, proximity, and mission. Parker Palmer stresses in *A Place Called Community* that community comes as a by-product of commitment and struggle.[17]

Occasionally, I attend Metro Church in Kelowna in the morning. It is a fascinating church within the Canadian Mennonite Brethren denomination. It has existed for several years as an outreach community to the needs of downtown residents, made up of a wide range of socioeconomic groups including the needy, homeless, addicts, and strugglers. The church ministers and counsels daily to so many human needs and feeds hundreds of them. I am able to attend in the morning when I can because my home church, called The Gathering of West Kelowna, is a fledging group that meets at five o'clock in the evening as a dinner church. It is led by my daughter, Heather Hitchcock. There are some similarities with Metro, as it follows the ministry explained in Verlon Fosner's *Dinner Church: Building Bridges by Breaking Bread*.[18]

Each Sunday as Metro Church begins its worship, it recites what is their longing of life together. They are beginning to grasp community.

> May the God who is community
> Be with us as we seek to be a community
>
> May God bless our dreams
> And may He shatter our dreams
> May God help us to be real

---

16. Jewish Roots 101, "Church of the Redeemer."
17. Palmer, *Place Called Community*, 16.
18. Fosner, *Dinner Church*, 22.

And to find depth in weakness and brokenness
May God help us to face and grow through conflict
Rather than pretend through being nice

May we look at each other through the soft eyes of respect and compassion
Rather than the hard eyes of criticism and condemnation
May God help us to let go of control and the need to fix one another

May God help us to discover that we are needy in our own souls
And give attention to our own hearts

May God shape us to be his people, until we resemble Christ
Who is full of mercy to the wicked and the ungrateful.

Amen.[19]

Belonging

A group at New Hope Baptist Church, to which I belonged in Victoria helped me to make an important decision in my life. I had learned to trust each one in the group to both have my back and to confront me with a challenge. I had come off my big motorcycle for the third time, only on this occasion it was serious. I was hospitalized with a broken leg in three places. At our midweek meeting, with my leg in a cast, I asked them to guide me as to whether I should give up the bike. They said they would pray and get back to me in a couple of weeks. I stood ready to do whatever they said. I had initiated my trust in them. Two weeks later they said not to give up my bike. *Life together* is not a cult where we are told what to do and think, but it is a belonging to which we are freely able to be accountable and committed.

There are principles that seem to enhance community among us as believers. Two, in particular, seem to work in the life of a local church. One is *giftedness*, the other is *goals* (or *mission*).

Giftedness (Charismata)

To single some churches out as charismatic is a misnomer because church is, by definition, a collection of people who are meant in some way to

---

19. Metro Church, "Community Prayer."

express their giftedness. All churches in this sense are meant to be charismatic. This contributes so much to a meaningful life together, where each can express their contribution and be affirmed and feel they belong. This is a far cry from church being just a Sunday gathering of people in an auditorium, featuring only a very few expressions of spiritual ability.

Trinity Baptist Church in Winnipeg, where I once served, had fallen on hard times and had few people. They were close to closing the church when I arrived with my family. Part of the transformation, growth, and ministry of this church as it revitalized was the attitude of those who had hung in even while the church declined. They accepted the need to change, which came not because of novel ideas or programs but because of a fresh work of the Spirit among us and an understanding of life together based on spiritual giftedness.

Spiritual (and practical) gifts, what the New Testament names as *charismata*, mean that each person is given gifts by the Holy Spirit to be lived out among those in community. The uppermost imagery is of the human body and the cohesive functioning of its parts to the benefit of all. Other helpful imagery of each making a valuable contribution could be that of a garden in which the gardener works to nurture each plant. A symphony orchestra is an interesting model of life together that well suits Christians seeking meaningful church life. The conductor seeks to guide the gifted instrumentalists or choristers into a harmonious expression of music. There is a particular bonding when the biblical emphasis of shared gifts and the development of spiritual gifts for all people is the uppermost goal of believers being together. This was my experience and joy at the churches I served. It was a joy (and work) for me to mentor and coach others to do the work of the ministry instead of doing it all myself. People began to feel empowered and worthwhile.

In true community, each person grows in confidence that he or she is a significant member of a larger entity. Of all people, the church must be able to give this message to its members.[20] God has accepted us; we must accept one another. Trinity Church became known as a place of acceptance among what I had affectionately named the motley crew; people who had been sidelined elsewhere or ignored began to trickle in. One such person was Heather Gavin, who had formed a mini community of female liturgical dancers who lived together in what was called the "White House" (because

---

20. "Those parts of the body that seem to be weaker are indispensable, and the parts that we think are less honorable we treat with special honor" (1 Cor 12: 22–23a).

that was the color of it). One day, she came to me timorously, because of so many rejections by other leaders, and asked if it would be possible to share a little of her ministry during a service. When I said, "Why not?" she burst into tears. That was the beginning of a beautiful ministry that enhanced our worship. That was not the only contribution, as Doug and Jeannie Hallstead had creative gifts in drama, which proved so effective in adding to the theme of any Sunday or at points in the liturgical year such as Easter, Advent, and Christmas. One of our church ladies was married to a psychiatrist. One day he showed up to church with her, the day we featured the banjo and a music group with guitars and drums—not the organ. I was fearful that he would dismiss us as weird. He didn't. Instead, he kept coming each Sunday and eventually made a confession of faith. I asked him why he had kept coming. His reply was that any group that could play banjo in worship had to be real enough for him to want to belong. More and more people began to experience freedom to express their talents and gifts and were released to teach, preach, counsel, organize care ministries, and pray for people to be healed in some way or other. Some learned to lead worship and, in that worship, be sensitive to the direction of God's Spirit. Don Butterworth, a chef and caterer, organized a crew to participate in what became our Wednesday evening version of what I had learned at the Church of the Redeemer in Houston. It was a night for the neighborhood, for the indigent, for distribution of needed clothes. Trinity had slowly grown into a place for such as these. We didn't need to teach about life together; we lived it, far from perfection but close to joy. Many people long for connection but end up marginalized, their gifts overlooked, their potential contributions lost. Trinity had slowly grown into a place for such as these.

Another aspect of Trinity, and other churches which I helped to lead, was our constant going to retreats to learn, grow with each other, and come closer to the Lord. These times away could be by camping or at retreat centers. Long hours spent together fostered community in a deep way.

Goals (Mission)

Those in community see their life together as involvement in some form of goal or mission. A secular illustration can be like a high school theater group that starts out in September hardly knowing each other but end up as a genuine community who relate to each other at a deep level by the time the school play is presented. During the school year, while intermingling with each other, their particular focus and relationships develop more keenly around their practises, rehearsals, making sets, and all that involvement in presenting the play. During this time, they experience effort, struggle, frustration, even tension, as well as hope and encouragement amid the hard work. It all culminates in the final closing night. When the school theater company meets for its wrap-up banquet, it has become more than a company—it is a community.

When I lived in Victoria, I joined a small group who gained a concern (mostly through the care of the women in the group) for the dreadful life of the prostitutes that trolled the streets of downtown Victoria. The women made sure the "girls" were warm on the cold nights by getting them winter clothes, were fed, and were protected from violence, all under the watchful eye of the men in the group, who let the pimps know that we were around to protect the "girls." Eventually, a couple of the girls escaped their sad life. The story is much more complex, but my point is that because our group was born in mission, it deepened our relationships, and whenever we met, we didn't need some program to tell us what to do. Prayer was intense and spontaneous. When there was good news about the "girls," we couldn't prevent ourselves from joyful worship. We were driven to the Scripture to wait on God for insight and answers to things that challenged us. We were such novices in what we were doing, but we were growing in our understanding of community that involved mission.

We need to understand that God himself is a community (the Trinity) and a missional God. When speaking to Zacchaeus in Luke 19:10, Jesus says, "The Son of Man came to seek and to save the lost." The goal is not fellowship per se but a place where, together, believers are helped to sense acceptance and belonging, brought about by their empowerment because of their giftedness and a common goal of spiritual development. Whatever the context, mission is part of life together.

APPENDIX

Books

- Alan J. Roxburgh's *Joining God, Remaking Church, Changing the World: The New Shape of the Church in Our Time* has outlined some important principles and practices to help this journey
- Mark Sayers, *Disappearing Church: From Cultural Relevance to Gospel Resilience*

- Peter Block, *Community: The Structure of Belonging*
- Parker J. Palmer, *A Place Called Community*
- John McKnight and Peter Block, *The Abundant Community: Awakening the Power of Families and Neighborhoods*
- Dietrich Bonhoeffer, *Life Together: The Classic Exploration of Christian Community*
- Lesslie Newbigin, *The Open Secret: An Introduction to the Theology of Mission*

Newbigin said that "the only hermeneutic of the gospel is a congregation of men and women who believe it and live by it."[21]

A further encouragement is to be found in The Commons Network, a "group of people committed to launching 'Communities of Hope,'" including members from Forge, The Missional Network, and the Northumbrian Collective.[22] When people feel called to form such a community of *life together*, they will need to understand that their main goal is to express Christ's life in the world. Setting out together, it will inevitably mean that they face the principles outlined by S. Murray in *Church After Christendom*, in which he discusses options for belonging in a community. Wherever we are, we must find ways of including those among whom God is working.[23]

---

21. Newbigin, *Gospel in a Pluralistic Society*, 227.
22. Commons Network, "Who Are We?"
23. Murray, *Church After Christendom*.

CHAPTER 5

Worship and Devotion

The true worshipers will worship the Father in the Spirit and in truth, for they are the kind of worshipers the Father seeks.

—JOHN 4:23

I DELIBERATELY PLACED THE topic of community before that of worship because I believe that the former is the context for the latter. Worship is about what God does to his people by his Spirit. In my lifetime, I have attended worship services in many forms and sizes all around the world. The impact of Black American and African American church worship and churches of Asian believers can be as profound as they are unique to one raised in a white Christian culture. From various years and times and places, I highlight in this chapter some memories to show the breadth and scope of worship. As in all topics in this book, this chapter is not about theory; head knowledge about kissing doesn't compare with the experience. So it is with worship; it cannot be only about knowledge, about how to do it or a commitment to a particular liturgical form or lack thereof. As I noted in the introduction of this book, stories in and of themselves do not express or deny the importance of doctrine or tradition. There are indeed important theological premises that are not ignored by my stories, for they are simply meant to show the heart, dynamic, and variety of worship that I have observed and experienced. Vibrant, creative, Spirit-empowered, transforming worship is a vital expression of Matt 6:33.

STORIES

Early Years

Growing up in England, I was raised the kind of Anglican that had a "hatch, match, and dispatch" allegiance to church. By this I mean we went to church for christenings, marriages, and funerals. I was blessed with a good singing voice and sang at my elementary school concerts. When I got to the Liverpool Collegiate, I was chosen to be in the soprano/treble section of the choir that sang Handel's *Messiah*. This was a six-month experience followed the next year by Haydn's *Creation*. Both events involved full orchestra, massed choir, esteemed soloists, and a huge organ (which was part of our daily school assembly and worship). It is virtually impossible to experience these things without getting some form of worship into your soul.

As I entered my teens, I accepted a role, for some pocket money, as a chorister at the procathedral choir of St. Chad's Church, Everton. For three years until I was fifteen, I learned the old liturgy of the Anglican church and sang various ancient choral pieces. I was no sissy, despite all this churchy stuff. In the meantime, I played soccer for the collegiate school First XI, and for a local boys team called Stardale United. Soccer was my first love. Except for my school studies and the usual escapades of male teenagers, like stealing pies from the local bake shop or breaking windows of the neighbors or setting fire to wooded areas or a street fight with other gangs (rather mild by today's standards), my life was that of a typical Liverpool working-class lad until I went to that weekend at Barnston Dale and entered a life of faith in Christ. A seed for worship had been planted in my soul and for the rest of my Christian life. I was to experience so many different expressions of worship. My emphasis in this chapter is mostly upon public worship without in any way minimizing private or personal worship. I will share insights later on about Isa 6 and the value of private experiences of worshiping. I realize that public worship on Sunday, for example, is only one of the options for many churches who have midweek gatherings of various numbers and who participate in worship in some form. Personal devotions to God ought to spill over from our soul when the community gathers. Liturgy and leadership have a role to play, but the involvement of the whole gathered community is uppermost.

Worship and Devotion

First Love

My journey into faith in the first four months after my conversion involved riding my bicycle each weekend to Bethshan Tabernacle Pentecostal Church, Whalley Range, Manchester. I was introduced to Pentecostal worship. Bethshan was a huge church by British standards at the time. It was full of young people who truly loved Jesus. Much singing was spontaneous and stirred the emotions. One sensed the presence of God in many ways. When winter came and bike riding was out, I became a member of the little Orrell Park Baptist Church in Liverpool. In their congregation was the same genre of young people excited about their faith. Worship was informal but also open to the Lord's presence, different but just as vital as the Pentecostal Church in Manchester. In August of that year, I went with this young peoples' group to a week's retreat at Hildenborough Hall in Frinton, a seaside town in Essex on the east coast of England (I told the story in chapter 2). At the end of the week of studies, we were invited to attend a midnight service in the thirteenth-century church to worship God. We met mostly in silence with occasional readings and prayers. Then came the invitation to be open to God and be guided by the Holy Spirit as to my future in life. I clearly heard a call to Christian ministry. When the service was over, I went alone to the shore on the North Sea facing Holland miles away. As I walked on the sand in the night with the waves gently washing over my feet, I sensed a call to go to Canada to renew my education, find a university, and study for the ministry. (That classical/traditional approach to Christian leadership was all I knew at the time. I have a different view of leadership now which I will share in the next chapter.) I had truly worshiped that night, been touched by God, and the direction of my life had been set.

I have shared in chapter 2 of my arrival in Canada and subsequent experiences. After a summer with Bill Mason, the famous Canadian canoeist at an InterVarsity Camp on the Manitoba / United States border, I headed for Oshawa by bus through the United States, where I studied in preparation for university. There I met Brenda, my wife now for sixty-two years. I attended her Calvary Baptist Church, a large and mostly working-class congregation in a General Motors town. What I remember profoundly was the evening services that were mostly a matter of singing gospel songs and hymns. The people sang with a depth of commitment to God and with full heart and faith. They were thrilling evenings to me. There are few non-charismatic churches where one can describe Christian worship as thrilling. To be fair, I recognize that these wonderful services represented only one aspect of worship. I was to experience such joy of congregational singing several times during my years of life and ministry. One example in that time was in the Royal Albert Hall in London, England, when the massed Welsh choirs sang traditional hymns such as "Guide Me, O Thou Great Jehovah," "O the Deep, Deep Love of Jesus," and "I Will Sing the Wondrous Story," etc.[1] The audience may not have been at church in the traditional sense, but God was worshiped through the power of song in a huge way!

I cannot share all my experiences of great singing, such as the years I spent at a Mennonite congregation in Vancouver, where the people sang like the Welsh do. How wonderful worship in that tradition was to me in those years. The following story from Canada expresses the duality of powerful worship, resultant ministry, and the gifts of God.

God's Power

David Watson was an Oxford scholar and Anglican clergyman who, at the time of this story, was developing an important ministry in the UK. His leadership at St. Michael le Belfrey in York had seen a failing church be renewed and eventually attracted a large congregation, as well as large gatherings at universities. Well-known musicians such as Andrew Maries, who wrote, *One Heart, One Voice*, a book about biblical worship for our day and age, came to serve at St. Michael's as one of the creative and influential team.[2] David had created a team to assist him in his "missions" in British towns, churches, and universities, as well as around the world. It consisted of singers and dancers but mostly actors who illustrated the themes about which he would talk.

Another leading musician who was at St. Michael's during this period was Graham Kendrick, one of the UK's leading evangelical song writers. Together with Roger Forster, Gerald Coates, and Lynn Green, he was a founder of the March for Jesus (a crowd-singing mission in many towns in the UK). He was based at St. Michael's in the late 1970s and was involved in student and university ministry. I met David about a year before I returned to England to be pastoral leader at Millmead Baptist Church in Guildford. David had been invited to Vancouver and the West Coast to lead his team in city missions. I met him there for the first time when I had come from

---

1. "Guide Me, O Thou Great Jehovah" by William Williams; "O the Deep, Deep Love of Jesus" by S. Trevor Francis; "I Will Sing the Wondrous Story" by Francis Rowley.

2. Maries, *One Heart, One Voice*.

Winnipeg to observe his missions. He came to Victoria for an evening rally at an Anglican church. I met him again before the start of the meeting. His team and several other local leaders gathered for prayer. I was asked to join them. As we prayed, I heard beautiful music and powerful singing and praise going on in the sanctuary, where hundreds had gathered. I assumed it was a young singing group leading the praise. When we entered the sanctuary after prayer, I discovered that those leading the praise were two ladies in their seventies. They knew how to sense the Holy Spirit and led worship accordingly. David spoke that evening on the infilling of the Holy Spirit. I was personally impacted and wanted to join those who were going for prayer after the service, but David asked me to take a group into the Lady Chapel to minister to some of those responding. Reluctantly, but drawn by God, I accepted and went with a small group into the little adjacent chapel.

I prayed for several, all the while fearful of my lack of skill. Then came the last request. This man was joined by a group of supporters. His request was that I would offer a "word of knowledge" to help him discern his future ministry. I knew nothing about the man and not much about a "word of knowledge." He felt it important that I not know his story. In trepidation I prayed something like this, "Lord, help this man to decide to accept economic loss by undertaking a ministry that will change his work schedule." When I ended my prayer, wanting to jump through the stained-glass windows, he looked at me and said that he was a pharmacist but felt called to minister with the folks who had come with him that night, to a needy children's care ministry in the afternoons. He would have to switch his pharmacy work to the evening at a substantial financial loss. My prayer by the Holy Spirit had sorted the matter out, and he and his companions rejoiced at the outcome. For my part, having experienced God at work in the worship service only minutes before, I had now seen it had affected me so that I was able to risk and be open to God myself. I realized anew that evening that there is a difference to ministry when it is led by the Holy Spirit. Life and ministry can be ordinary, but at times when worship is so alive, we can be helped to a fresh openness to God. Over the years, I have seen God work this way in many churches in various denominations.

Touched by the Spirit

Before I left for England, I had invited David and his team to Winnipeg, to do a city mission. It was held for three days at Rainbow Stage in the park, which is one of the largest outdoor theaters in Canada. The dance, drama, and singing, followed by David's preaching, impacted people in the city, including Trinity Baptist Church where I was pastoral leader. One Sunday after that event, we had a remarkable but not untypical service at Trinity. Gilbert Patterson had been at the church for forty years and supported its conservative and traditional approach. He was very leery of the new things coming to the church since I had arrived. He was a faithful man of fine character. He had asked me to let him lead a morning service. In fear and trepidation, I said yes because I knew that God had touched his life in the past months. I sat with my family that morning, as I always did, until it was my turn to preach. Gilbert let the singing group start the service, but after a few songs to a seemingly enthused congregation, he quietly said, "Let us stop and pause. I believe there is a spirit of depression among us with which God wants to deal." I wanted to crawl under the pew. I knew that we had arranged for the dance team and a very excellent drama to precede my earth-changing sermon (just kidding about the sermon). There was a long silence broken by Anne Barnland, who shared the story of her husband's cancer and how they had both been deeply depressed during the week. Ken Voth, an elder, spoke of depressive Scriptures that had come to him during the week. He was puzzled but now understood why and shared them. Over the next half hour, others shared their experiences of depression and sadness in their lives. Then Tannis McBurney, who had a beautiful voice, broke out in the simple song (Tannis was not on the music team that day, but God directed her to sing). Tears began to flow in the congregation and then, without my direction or anyone else's, small groups of people gathered to minister and pray for one another. Gilbert sheepishly came over to me and asked what he should do. I said we do nothing except watch the Lord at work. At about the two-hour mark, we began quietly singing a few songs, and then the service wound down. We had no drama, dance, sermon, or anything else that morning, but we had an experience of God in public much like Isaiah had experienced in private (Isa 6).

Each year from Maundy Thursday evening to Easter Saturday evening, our whole church went to a nearby retreat center to be together as a congregation and to experience God's blessing upon our corporate lives. We held worship that involved foot washing and a time of confession and repentance. As well as biblical sessions about the meaning of Easter, we held a special communion service that lasted up to three hours as we waited on God, experienced prayer for each other, and experienced healing and restoration. We returned home by Saturday evening, spiritually fresh for worship on Easter Sunday morning.

Once a month at Trinity, we held communion, and the whole service was devoted to it in liturgical style. People came to the front to receive the bread and wine. The elders and others served the elements but also did more; they offered ministry to those wanting it. This could take time; people were helped, blessed, and healed. Here was a time for confession, forgiveness, and restoration, such as cannot happen when communion is a quick appendage to a morning service. Worship ought to lead us to experience God in meaningful ways.

I did return to England with my family. Soon after I arrived, to my deep sadness and pain, Belfry Trust, who gave oversight to David Watson's ever-expanding ministry and mission, came to see me in Guildford. David had taken seriously ill with cancer. Millmead Church, aware of the impact of David's ministry around Britain, released me for about a week each month to take his place in leading missions around the UK with his creative team. I remained pastoral leader at Millmead during this very busy time. I learned so much about the use of the arts in worship. I did this for almost a year before David died.

Liturgy Live

Let me return to the story of the Episcopal Church of the Redeemer, Houston. Part of the strength of their worship was their community life during the week, which meant that many were involved in the worship, and their ability to use liturgy creatively in openness to the Holy Spirit was profoundly evident. The people would share stories of God at work in their lives during the past week, and those stories were powerful. The choir did not mostly sit up in areas removed from the congregation but among the people or walking the aisles, encouraging and assisting in worship, including congregational singing. Such openness to God's Spirit was always there whenever I attended St. Michael le Belfrey, York, or Holy Trinity Brompton, London.

Much of what I have shared above was also part of the worship life of Millmead Baptist Church, where I was called after Winnipeg. It had become one of the largest Baptist churches in the UK at that time under the leadership of David Pawson. His powerful preaching drew crowds of people also to the evening service, as they looked for vitality and biblical truth not much available in their own churches in morning services. Guildford is a conservative, wealthy area in the Bible Belt of southern England. The church had a lot of talent, and several national celebrities attended the church but that was only a small part of its impetus. God's Spirit had visited the church in unique ways years before I arrived. Also, in its long history it had developed a deep spirituality about its life and leadership. The people loved God and his gospel.

When I arrived at the church, much was already in place for what I experienced most weeks. We had an organ, grand piano, small orchestra, men's singing group, occasional choir, and several superb soloists. Numerous folks in the music area were prominent leaders in places such as the BBC and other London musical and choral groups. As I settled in, there were emerging drama and dance groups. The congregation knew how to sing so well, and while blessed by its musicians, they could sing powerfully in a cappella. This was wonderful indeed, but it was not the major essence of the church I was to lead. Millmead had been touched by the British charismatic movement of the seventies and eighties and was open to the Holy Spirit in so many parts of its life. Also, by tradition, leadership of its services was shared among other gifted people (I rarely led the services). David Pawson had continued in his preaching, and so the church had this wonderful balance of traditional and orthodox life, as well as manifestations of the Holy Spirit. I simply enjoyed what I had inherited. On most Sundays we would start by singing; some of the songs and hymns were pre-chosen, but other songs came spontaneously from the congregation. The same was often true about our prayers. Perhaps the service leader would speak a prayer, but then the congregation would pray. What a mixture that could be: slightly formal, well-said prayers, utterances in tongues, and prophetic words. The elders had developed a policy not to respond immediately to the professed prophecies but to record them and have them printed the following week in the bulletin with a note by the elders who would either express that they were prophetic, and the church should follow, or that they were merely encouraging words to bless the congregation. Perhaps best of all, the joyful prayers of so many would ring out in the sanctuary by simple down-to-earth people who loved God so deeply. One of those people was Harold Wakeford, an elderly gardener whose prayers, in a booming voice, would sound something like this (I can't possibly replicate the beauty of his spirit and prayers despite my attempt to do so below):

> O Lord, what a smashing morning it is; the beautiful sunshine and the bees buzzing and all those fabulous flowers. The rose, Lord, it

is so intricately woven, just like we are. O Lord and you are beautiful also! You shine in our hearts, and we are so happy... happy... happy to know You. We love you, Lord. We love each other in this church. Lord, we need you. May your Spirit come in power in this service. Hallelujah, hallelujah.

Many people in the church had training in simple counseling for spiritual issues, so often after service, there would be groups ministering to others. One Sunday, the BBC decided to broadcast our service nationally. We did not put on anything special that morning; we had the dance and drama ministries and creative reading of Scripture with visual background. Our time was limited to one hour because of the BBC broadcast, but we sang so well, and my sermon was quite short. We ended with a very enthusiastic congregation singing, "You Shall Go Out with Joy."[3] When I got home with the family for lunch, I got a long-distance call from Alan McNally. He was calling to say that those many years ago when he was one of the four lads who had gone to Barnston Camp, where I had been led to Christ, he also quietly had made the same commitment. He had become a naval officer and had that morning discovered my journey. I wept.

In the next chapter on leadership, I will share a story of a Millmead evening service of baptism in which the Lord worked remarkably in worship, and how that relates to effective leadership. My main influences in worship have come from Baptist/Anabaptist, Anglican, Charismatic, and Celtic communities, but also I have experienced deep worship around the world in a variety of denominations and movements.

BEYOND OURSELVES

I want to now take you on a journey that will display the many facets of public worship in addition to what I have shared above. For many, these stories will be outside the realm of their experience. They are not in chronological order or in any priority. Let's begin in St. Petersburg, Russia, where I flew for a three-day break while lecturing east of Moscow. I visited the Hermitage Museum and saw the famous painting of the *Prodigal Son*, after which I went to St. Isaacs. The beauty of the building and the magnificence of the icons were in themselves a worshipful experience enjoyed by the hundreds walking around. I stayed there a long time and attended a Russian Orthodox wedding, with all its pageantry and vestments. This is public worship

3. Written by Steffi Geiser Rubin and Stuart Dauermann.

of great beauty; it was more than a ceremony. After the wedding I walked around the choir area where men were singing Orthodox hymns, preparing for a service that night. The power of their voices and the beauty of their traditional singing rang throughout the vast building, as if to glorify God. Just before the evening service, hundreds lined up to make confessions to a priest. I came away touched by public worship in a new way. I need to add this point regarding the emerging number of churches (Fresh Expressions, dinner church, et al.) that center their time together around a dinner or some such meal. One cannot fit the plethora of things I have noted above about worship into a single service on a Sunday, or other time. Means need to be found for believers to experience worship in some of the ways that I have stated. Worship is a driving force and a foundation for being the kind of community that attracts and sustains those who become part of us.

Once while in Paris on All Hallows' Eve (what Canadians call Halloween in a huge distortion of its real meaning), I first visited the outer courtyard of Notre Dame Cathedral late in the afternoon. About fifty trees had been erected representing many countries—e.g., Canadian maple and fir. On one tree was a note attached (I forget the exact words, but it went something like this): "Respect this and all trees because on a tree Christ died for mankind." The next day was to be All Saints' Day (hence the term like Christmas Eve—All Hallows' or Saints' Eve). Across Europe it is a national holiday, and there are many church services. I went into Notre Dame, where a beautiful service was being held. On All Saints' Eve two years later, I went to Canterbury Cathedral in England to attend a Requiem Mass. Some of it was beyond me, but Mozart, Bach, and Handel's contribution to worship is worth its weight in gold. Another powerful memory comes from a downtown Catholic church in Rio de Janeiro near Copacabana Beach, Brazil. I went there on my way home to Canada after ministering for a couple of weeks at a favela. Their 7:00 a.m. Simple Mass was crowded with people in their twenties and thirties. I didn't understand Portuguese, but I knew the language of the Spirit. God's spirit was present in an amazing way. I sought out the priest at the end of the service, and we talked and embraced as I said to him, "Surely God was in this place." What I noticed in Rio was common in all my stories about worship, namely the almost 100 percent participation by those attending. There were no spectators, no sit-and-soak mentality. Another memory of this was at the Notre Dame University chapel in Indiana where, during Mass, there was such involvement and joy when singing "I Am the Bread of Life" by Suzanne Toolan.

Worship and Devotion

Etched in my memory forever will be the gathering of pastors from behind the Iron Curtain in Eastern Europe, before the Berlin Wall came down. We had all met furtively in the Lutheran Mission of Dr. Paul Toaspern. (I will relate the story of Dr. Toaspern in the next chapter on leadership.) We were European church leaders gathered to help plan Acts 86 at the Birmingham National Conference Centre in England, involving John Wimber, Michael Green, and others—a conference of renewal for Europe. Michael Harper and I were the Brits on the organizing committee. We had walked from the Brandenburg Gate border crossing to Paul Toaspern's Lutheran Mission to meet for the day. We were planning for many pastors and leaders to come from Eastern Europe to the meetings in Birmingham. We were worshiping God when everyone began to "sing in the Spirit," and I understood the day of Pentecost in a new way.

Celtic Worship

Come now with me to Tobermory on the Isle of Mull in the Hebrides Islands, off the western coast of Scotland. At the most southern tip of the Mull is a tiny but famous island called Iona. Here St. Columba went from Ireland in AD 563 as a missionary to Scotland and Britain. Because of my Celtic studies, I know the following story well:

> Lying off the west coast of the Isle of Mull the tiny Isle of Iona, barely three miles long by one mile wide, has had an influence out of all proportion to its size on the establishment of Christianity in Scotland, England and throughout mainland Europe. Iona's place in history was secured in 563 AD when St. Columba arrived on its white sandy beaches with 12 followers, built his first Celtic church and established a monastic community. Once settled, the Irish monk set about converting most of pagan Scotland and northern England to the Christian faith. Iona's fame as a missionary centre and outstanding place of learning eventually spread throughout Europe, turning it into a place of pilgrimage for several centuries to come. Iona became a sacred isle where kings of Scotland, Ireland and Norway were buried.[4]

My family was living in Guildford near London at the time, and we had gone to Tobermory on the Isle of Mull for Christmas. We worshiped on Christmas Eve at the local Presbyterian kirk. Two days later, I drove

---

4. Johnson, "St Columba."

down to the tip of Mull, got the little ferry to Iona, and visited the Iona Celtic Community that lived there and practiced Christian Celtic worship. Several weeks later, I traveled to the tidal island (called Holy Isle) of Lindisfarne, just off the eastern coast of Northern England near Newcastle. On the island is St. Mary the Virgin parish church (originally built AD 635). There was an important center of Celtic Christianity under Saints Aidan and Cuthbert. Ray Simpson founded a community there about forty years ago, known for its Celtic worship and monastic life. His book *Exploring Celtic Worship* and the community website will help one understand the Celtic community life and worship.[5] Across on the other side of England near the west coast is the Northumbrian Community at Nether Springs which affords a similar experience of Celtic life and worship.[6] I have visited these three communities and experienced the depth of Celtic worship there and in several Celtic churches in Europe and North America.

Taizé

I was too old to be allowed attendance at the Taizé (in France) annual community gathering because the demand among the young people is immense. I have had to settle for CDs of their music, videos of their worship, and attendance at several of the local churches that offer Taizé worship in North America.

> The Taizé Community is an ecumenical Christian monastic fraternity in Taizé, France. It is composed of more than one hundred brothers, from Catholic and Protestant traditions, who originate from about thirty countries around the world. It was founded in 1940 by Brother Roger Schütz, a Reformed Protestant. Taizé has become one of the world's most important sites of Christian pilgrimage, with a focus on youth. Over 100,000 young people from around the world make pilgrimages to Taizé each year for prayer, Bible study, sharing, and communal work. Through the community's ecumenical outlook, they are encouraged to live in the spirit of kindness, simplicity and reconciliation.[7]

---

5. Simpson, *Exploring Celtic Spirituality*; Simpson, "Introducing."
6. See https://www.northumbriacommunity.org/ for more detail.
7. Wikipedia, "Taizé Community."

Tradition

Tradition is the live faith left to us by those who have died, while traditionalism can be the dead faith of many who are still alive today.

Over the years in various places, I have attended Choral Evensong, which takes place around five o'clock in the evening on weekday afternoons in many Anglican churches in the UK. This is a brief service of Scripture readings, collects, prayers, and a choir singing a particular piece. On one such occasion, I was in Norwich Cathedral, England, when at the close of the service, the vicar quietly announced that the service marked eight hundred years since Evensong in some form had been held there.

Life and ministry can be ordinary at times; we cannot always live or worship on highs (and hence the value of thoughtful liturgy and live tradition), but when worship is so alive, we can be helped to a fresh openness to God. Worship as Isaiah experienced it in Isa 6:1–9 should be transformative. Tradition, when experienced in the spirit of heartfelt worship, is a beautiful thing, and we reject it at our loss. To be present in King's College Chapel, Cambridge, to hear *Ave Verum Corpus* by Mozart prints an indelible mark on one's soul. Tradition, of course, is not only the possession of liturgical churches but of nonliturgical gatherings also; I can recall Christmas Eve services in an evangelical church as the worshipers held candles and sang "Cantique de Noël" (O Holy Night). There are many other stories of the power of tradition, but my concern here is that we learn in our local churches to create traditions in worship wherever we assemble and see their value as we do family traditions in our homes.

Our Contemporary Struggle

It is important for me to share my joy in some of the more contemporary worship experiences of recent years. At the same time, I am concerned that what is really needed beyond a *seeker sensitive* emphasis is *Spirit sensitive* worship. We must be careful about studying what consumers want rather than what God does. As life in the culture becomes more superficial, the temptation is to make worship the same. As I write, I am aware of and moved by some of the wonderful singing by churches such as Bethel ("Goodness of God") in Reading, California, and Hillsong Church ("King of Kings" and "What a Beautiful Name") in Australia.[8] Other compos-

---

8. "Goodness of God" by Jenn and Brian Johnson; "King of Kings" by Brooke and

ers such as Matt Redman ("10,000 Reasons") offer worship of the highest order. A new generation is more naturally disposed to Corey Voss and spiritual songs such as his "Praise the King." Such contemporary expressions in worship exist also in many churches, retreats, and other annual worship and teaching conferences. The Pentecostal/Charismatic movement has been a force for such power in a particular aspect of worship, particularly among youth over the last fifty years. The impact on youth culture has been amazing, with thousands coming to faith in Christ. This cannot be dismissed lightly, despite a few leaders who have abused and damaged people in some of the churches and organizations involved. There are churches that have kept alive both tradition and historic liturgy but are doing so in the context of the contemporary culture and with both an openness to the ministry of the Holy Spirit and the understanding of the need for change in the church. One excellent example is Holy Trinity Brompton, London, UK.[9]

What grips me for today's church is not so much a particular form of so-called contemporary worship or the expression of any one generation, but the reality that there are basics to worship that flow through the centuries and are contained in Scripture. It is those basics that count the most in any worship experience (I try to outline them in the next section). It is not my place to critique contemporary expressions of worship through the lens of my generation or background but to look for how, in their own way, this generation of believers is expressing those basics for the glory of God.

INSIGHTS

A Little Theology

"Worship is a way of life not a 'thing' that we do," said A. W. Tozer.[10] He also wrote, "Worship is the missing jewel in the Evangelical crown."[11] The place to begin is not with method or theory but with understanding of the biblical nature of worship.

Scott Ligertwood and Jason Ingram; "What a Beautiful Name" by Brooke Ligertwood and Ben Fielding.

9. Holy Trinity Brompton, "Our Story."
10. Tozer, *Pursuit of God*, 87.
11. Tozer, "Worship," 96.

Worship and Devotion

This next paragraph is a generality; many churches are not like this, but there is an axiom in life that generalities are generally true. People like to worship in ways in which they feel comfortable, be they traditionalists with set liturgies, charismatics with extemporaneous liturgies, or evangelicals with their rather passive services, in which people speak or sing to them as they sit in the service. *The issue is not what we prefer but what God wants.* He calls for praise and adoration in worship (whatever its form or liturgy), which involves the whole being, led by the Spirit, rehearsing the gospel story.

Our goals in worship are:

- to honor him
- to respond to his love
- to express our love to him
- to bless him
- to allow him to bless us
- to affirm our faith
- to hear the voice of God
- to be motivated for service/ministry
- to experience existentially his presence and power

There are three fallacies we can make about public worship—namely, that it is about *place*, about *form*, or about *us*. In *Celebration of Discipline*, Richard Foster writes, "Worship is the human response to the divine initiative. Singing, praying, praising all may lead to worship, but worship is more than any of them. Our spirit must be ignited by the divine fire. As a result, we need not be overly concerned with the question of a correct form for worship. The issue of high liturgy or low liturgy, this form or that form is peripheral rather than central."[12] In a number of his writings, Foster stresses that worship is one of several spiritual disciplines for the Christian. Further insight to this theme can be gained through the Renovaré Institute for Christian Spiritual Formation.[13]

My observation is that whatever the denomination or liturgy, there is a tendency in many to reduce worship to singing and listening to a sermon.

---

12. Foster, *Celebration of Discipline*, 197–98.
13. Renovaré Institute, "About."

To understand worship is to see it in the paradigm of the rainbow or kaleidoscope: multicolored, multifaceted, and open to a range of possibilities and expressions. In the stories above about churches in which I served, there was always a blend of ancient and modern. Services would be creative in many ways, such as singing creeds written by contemporary writers or having Scripture read antiphonally, dramatized, or expressed by audiovisuals. There was always room for reflection, confession, poetry, and prayers, ancient and modern. There was an openness to God's Spirit, but there was also order. There was spontaneity among those in the congregation, and leadership and direction by discerning and gifted leaders. None of the churches had a regular weekly choir, but often choirs and choral groups were created for a particular purpose, often with very gifted soloists and musicians, as well as bands and orchestras in some instances. Drama and dance were expressed as part of creative liturgies. I realize, however, that one must work within the resources and giftedness available in a given church community, not try to copy well-financed churches. To use an old phrase, we need to cut the cloth to suit its measure, meaning that we have to work within the resources that we have, but we can be creative in whatever setting we find ourselves and be open to the serendipity of God's Spirit in our worship.[14]

The Celtic Christians of the fifth through eighth centuries were not dualists. Theirs was not the Greek mentality of splitting life into compartments. For the Celts there was no real division between work and worship, as many of their prayers and domestic liturgies reveal. Worship must be part of our daily lives if it is to be powerful in our public lives. When Matt 6:33 is a way of life for us, then a foundation for meaningful worship is laid. Sunday becomes the sum total of our daily experiences with God, not a place to get a fix or dutifully go through a ritual. Worship on Sunday, whatever the form or genre, comes powerfully alive when those attending bring to the event a life of private devotions with God, as well as a meaningful engagement with a spiritual community. This is not to say that there isn't a very important place for Sunday worship (or another special day) to be the event wherein God's Spirit visits his people in a special way through liturgy, community, giftedness, and serendipity.

---

14. Idiom Origins, "Cut One's Coat."

Worship and Devotion

Isaiah 6:1–9

Worship is not just about self-expression but about experiencing something transcendent, as Isaiah did. The experience of Isa 6:1–9 is recorded over and over in the Bible. Isaiah had seen God's glory (verses 1–4), received his grace (verses 5–7), and responded to his "go" (verses 8–9).[15] Isaiah's experience was remarkable. He was made to see wonder, and he experienced *awe*, not schlock or hype. He certainly could not have been bored. There were sights, sounds, and even smells; these activities and phenomena are not about noise per se but about the sensuous nature of worship. Catholic, Anglican, and Greek Orthodox churches all replicate this to some degree in their Masses/Eucharists.

Note the similarities of Isa 6 with the events at Pentecost in Acts 2. Worship in our culture has been reduced so often to entertainment, bereft of mystery. In both the Old and New Testaments, worship was seen as a demonstration of God's power either for battle or for witness. In the Epistles it is seen as a means of hearing from God and ministering the grace and healing of God to others.

Worship by its very nature must engage us. We may have brilliant bands and "worship" leaders, but sometimes they simply perform for us on the platform rather than lead us into the presence of God. We may have technology, but we may at the same time lack mystery or presence. Equally true is that traditional liturgies can be people merely going through the motions. Worship has rather to do with inviting others into the reality of our mystery, the gospel story, and the experience of God. What both liturgical and (some) charismatic churches offered was participation in essentially biblical expressions of prayer, gifts, communion, doctrinal profession with traditional or contemporary expressions of creeds, personal/public confession, and ministry that could extend to healing or hearing from God through ordinary believers.

---

15. Read Exod 15:1–21; Dan 7; the transfiguration in Matt 17; and Rev 4 and 5. Sally Morgenthaler writes, "Worship no longer means what it did in ancient times: a multisensory engagement with the God of the universe. Somewhere along the way, we abandoned the rich, Judeo foundation of sign, symbol, ritual, incense, and movement. We discarded the multifaceted gatherings of the early Christians: sacrament as splendid feasts, mind-sharpening odes to the triune God, unedited psalmody (we forget how familiar the early Christians were with grief), exuberant, spontaneous thanksgiving, and vibrant narrative." Morgenthaler, *Worship Evangelism*, 42.

Players on the Stage

In worship we are witnessing what an alternative society looks like. In true worship God is in control. In 1 Cor 14, Paul has a dual emphasis about worship when he essentially says to not control the Spirit and not be controlled by mere emotions. When we express ourselves physically in worship, our actions must match with what is happening in our hearts.[16] The use of drama, video, and technology in worship fits well into Isa 6, but only if what is behind such efforts is the deeper goal of helping people experience God, his gospel, and his truth. If we want to get truly serious about worship, then we can do no better than to be creative with liturgies that have meaning, mystery, history-remembrance (the continuous present), and truth attached to them. Those who don't remember family stories lose their identity; it is no different with church life. Kierkegaard said of worship that we are the players on the stage, and God is the audience seeing if we portray both him and his truth with joyous integrity.[17]

My own observation is that much of the genre of worship in nonliturgical evangelical churches omits the gospel themes of sin, repentance, forgiveness, assurance, hope, etc. because those themes are said to be not "seeker friendly."[18] However, those themes are part of the gospel, through which we can celebrate the reconciling work of the God we are worshiping. It is God, not the seeker or even the Christian, who is the subject and object of our worship. We can be creative, artistic, and even technological; however, we must not make our worship human centered. Rather, it must be God centered, in which the locus of authority is not us but, by the moving of God's Spirit on the truth of his word, is about himself to his people.

POINTS TO PONDER

My longing is that we learn to recover or establish intergenerational worship that grows out of intergenerational community. Charles Wesley's hymn "Jesus, the Name High over All" touches me in the same way as does Hillsong Church singing "What a Beautiful Name." We need to help one another realize that worship is a *priority*, a *privilege*, and a *power*.[19] The con-

---

16. Isaiah 6:5 reveals this.
17. Kierkegaard, *Purity*, loc. 151–52.
18. Hybels and Mittelberg, *Becoming a Contagious Christian*.
19. Worship is a *priority* (Rom 12:1–3), a *privilege* (Heb 10:19–25), and a *power* (1

Worship and Devotion

text of worship is the body of Christ, not an audience at a performance. It is a community of people expressing what they are living.[20] Community and worship are as inextricably bound as love and marriage.[21] My observation is that many churches give scant attention to planning worship, training worship leaders, or preparing diligently even for the coming Sunday. Planning is not opposite to being open to the Holy Spirit when we gather for worship.

Our goals in worship can be many. Here are a few.

We express our love to him in *praise* (Ps 100). Its physical forms are many, including singing, dancing, clapping, hand raising, and declaring things about God. We can also worship in *adoration*, which is devotion to God that says, "I Love You, Lord"[22] (its physical forms are also many, including kneeling, bowing, lying prostrate, and sitting in silence). Our worship in praise and adoration includes God's Spirit prodding us to minister to each other.[23] It is this part of worship that encourages and affirms the gifts of us all. God speaks through us in a variety of ways. We are all priests who minister to God and to each other. Once we grasp this, we come not just to get something out of the gathering but to give.

A Christmas cake has many ingredients. A book has many chapters and ideas. Biblical worship has many forms and expressions.[24] You won't be able to include them all each week, but they should, over time, be used in the life of the worshiping community. I question the necessity of having traditional preaching or repeating the same worship format every week. There are creative alternatives that keep alive our need and love for learning and knowing the Bible and the life it expresses. Once a month on Sunday, or whenever a worship gathering is held, we should create room for the arts in some form, and then (for nonliturgical churches) we should hold communion for the whole service on another Sunday (perhaps that is the Sunday to not have a sermon, for the Lord's table has so much Scripture to teach us that allows us to experience its message). What sometimes gets lost by all traditions is that at the Last Supper and in the book of Acts, this *service* was held in the context of a meal.[25] Every church has liturgy in some

---

Cor 14:25; Eph 5:18–20; Phil 3:3).

20. Ps 35:18; Acts 2:41–47; 1 Cor 14:22–26; Eph 5:18–21; 1 Pet 2:4–10.
21. Ps 100:3; 1 Cor 2:7; Eph 1:4–10; 1 Pet 2:9–10.
22. As expressed by Laurie Klein's song of the same name.
23. Deut 6:5; 1 Cor 14:24–26; Eph 5:18–20; 1 Pet 2:4–10.
24. Gen 1:1–27; Exod 19; Neh 9:1–6; John 1:1–5, 14; 1 Cor 14:1–33.
25. Acts 2:41–47; 1 Cor 11:17–34.

form; that liturgy can become dull and stale if we limit the ingredients to the same old routine, be it in a cathedral, a charismatic gathering, or some other form of traditional service.

To seek first the kingdom of God and his righteousness is how Christ wants us to live out our everyday discourse. Worshiping together as a community deepens our faith and expresses our hope in an often hopeless world. Our perspective on worship will determine our experience of it.

APPENDIX

Books

- Sally Morgenthaler, *Worship Evangelism: Inviting Unbelievers into the Presence of God*
- Gordon D. Fee, *Paul, the Spirit, and the People of God*
- Bob Rognlien, *Experiential Worship: Encountering God with Heart, Soul, Mind, and Strength*
- Eleanor Kreider and Alan Kreider, *Worship and Mission After Christendom*

CHAPTER 6

Leadership and Character

Fame is what you are known for; greatness is who you are.

—Sandra Zimmer[1]

I WRITE THIS CHAPTER, as a fellow struggler; I will share my strengths and weaknesses, successes and failures, as well as reflect on my convictions about leadership.

When I began this book, I knew that one day I would come to chapter 6 on leadership, and among the skills needed in a difficult task, character was a vital part of being a leader. I have come to believe deeply that part of character formation is the commitment to the lordship of Christ as expressed in Matt 6:33. I approach this chapter fearfully because it is a deeply personal matter. Perhaps the advantage of age (i.e., being elderly) is that one lets go of trying to prove or defend oneself. One realizes, too, the vital interconnection of leadership, personality, and character that can govern our ministries in church, family, and community.

I want to affirm my belief in the importance of leadership, regardless of the structure that contains it. The fundamental issue that gets lost as we continue the habits and forms of past generations is about what kind of leadership and what kind of leader is expressed in Scripture (the New Testament uses the word "leadership" sparingly). Books on leadership theory are legion, both in the secular world and in the church, but my concern is about the assumption of modernity that there are predictable principles of

1. Zimmer, "Famous," para. 4.

leadership to be followed that produce success. Jesus was instead the model of servant leadership.[2]

STORIES

Redwoods

Among the many trips I made with my motorcycle club was one that took us to the redwoods of California from Vancouver one July. On this occasion, I needed to stay in Vancouver until noon on Sunday while the club had left en masse on Saturday at noon. I began my journey a whole day after they left, and I hoped I could catch up to them by Monday evening. I stopped for a break around six o'clock in the evening. I got back on my bike, wasn't watching what I was doing, and alas within a few yards in the parking lot, I hit a concrete block and damaged my oil pan. It starting leaking badly, and I knew I could not go on. After hours of searching, I found two young mechanics who offered to work on my bike. I booked in to a local hotel and spent a lonely, anxious night. By noon the next day, I continued my trip, minus four hundred dollars for repairs and a big motel bill I hadn't planned for. I was now well over two days behind the others. I drove all the rest of that day, with only moments at rest stops. I caught up with the group near midnight and got little sleep before we all headed off next morning. It was a hot day, and I was very sleepy, which is not a good recipe for riding a big motorcycle at high speed. I fought all day to stay awake. It was a thoroughly miserable experience until that evening when we camped. The rest of the trip was fine. I got to see the glory of the Redwoods.

This story is somewhat a parable of my leadership. I set out on my motorcycle trip with good intentions, but on the journey I encountered setbacks through my own carelessness. I have in my ministry been genuine in seeking first the kingdom of God and his righteousness, but I have also been waylaid and sidetracked through various missteps.

Renewal

When I visited the Church of the Redeemer in Houston, Texas, I made a side trip to Galveston. While I was there, I discovered that the designer and builder of the seawall was Martyn Roberts, a brilliant US Army engineer.

2. 1 Thess 2:7–8, 11–12.

Leadership and Character

After being asked to lead a Baptist Church meeting, he experienced chaos and wrote in 1875 the now-famous and most used guide for conducting meetings with decorum and order titled, *Robert's Rules of Order*.[3] It became the norm for most institutions, both secular and religious. It has its value and place for conducting business, but it does not capture the heart of a kingdom community as did Acts 15, where consensus, prayer, and listening to the Holy Spirit seemed the order of their deliberations.

In this period, I was called to Trinity Baptist Church in Winnipeg as the pastoral leader. It was in a very discouraged and declining state when I arrived. Throughout the following years, it experienced a powerful renewal and transition and became an exciting kingdom community, full of creativity in all aspects of its life and worship. One evening soon after I arrived, there was to be a church business meeting (based on *Robert's Rules of Order*). The chairs were all in neat rows, and the conference table was set in place for the officials to conduct the business. Minutes of the previous meeting were read out and so on and so forth, except that the people were going through the motions to meet a scheduled institutional requirement. They had done this for years. I normally did not preside at church *business* meetings, but as the meeting dragged on, I asked permission to speak. I said something like this: "People, we are discouraged and struggling, and there are only a few of us. Let us set our seats in a circle, do away with the official table, suspend the agenda, and let's simply sit around and talk to each other about our fears, hurts, and longings. Let us pray together and for each other. We are not city hall; we are a community of fellow strugglers and children of the King."

We did this, and we were all blessed. I suggested to the one who had prepared to moderate the *business* that we briefly conclude what we needed to do by consensus. He agreed. It took a further ten minutes, and one joyful little congregation went home. That evening paved the way for another event two weeks later when I was officially inducted into my ministry at the church. All the ceremonies with pomp and circumstance were conducted in the beautiful sanctuary with its stained-glass windows and organ (reflecting the British roots of the church's beginning almost a century before). Religious and civic leaders were there. At the end of the ceremony, we went to the lower hall for refreshments. Jack Farr, the local area minister for the denomination and a good friend, called people together for the grace to be said. Jack intoned, "Now the Reverend Roxburgh will say the grace." After

---

3. Robert, *Robert's Rules*.

a pregnant pause, I gently but firmly said, "Jack, my name is Bob. I won't say the grace for tonight because we must not see me as the paid chaplain of events but as a leader among equals, most of whom are quite capable of saying the grace. May I ask one of the congregation to say the grace?" Someone did, and we ate happily, and the renewal of Trinity Church had begun. The years that followed produced such joy, as I watched people grow in their own gifts, leadership, and ministries.

Millmead, England

When I write about leadership at Millmead, I am writing beyond ideas of "ministerial staff"; I am writing about the life of many of the congregation in some form. I inherited this as I arrived at Millmead and developed it further during my years at the church. One of my strengths was the desire and ability to empower others for ministry.

Elders

The elders were deeply respected by the congregation because of the process of choosing them for the nature of their lives and their spiritual discernment. It has been many years since I left Millmead, but recently Brenda and I attended the memorial service of one of those elders by Zoom. Amid the testimony to his life was the anecdote of part of the selection process of elders in his day. According to 1 Tim 3 and Titus 1, this involved going to his place of employment to enquire of his reputation. This was no filling in of numbers for a church board; this was a recognition of the worth and character of the elder, which had earned trust of the congregation and outsiders over years. Elders were called after a protracted process of prayer and sharing among the house groups and congregational meetings (see below).

Because of its size, the church was divided into five geographic neighborhoods called "congregations." Each had neighborhood pastors and house group leaders who assisted the elders within those neighborhoods. (None of these ministries involved paid positions.) Hence, the flow was elders, neighborhood pastors, and house group leaders. Writing about this leadership flow will explain a story that I relate below about leadership in a down-to-earth way. The major effect of this structure was to involve many people in leadership and offer adequate pastoral care to all. The joy for me was that I never felt that I had to be in charge of everything but that I was part of a team that cared for and ministered to the congregation. I rarely led worship, as it was done by those gifted to do so, but I did show up to the Tuesday night gathering of all those involved in the coming Sunday worship to offer help and insight if needed. The English tradition of both morning and evening services allowed numbers of others to preach. Weddings, funerals, and baptisms were shared among all the leaders as was appropriate at the time. Pastoral care was given by those in leadership in the congregations. This paragraph above lays the groundwork for my next story.

Guy Fawkes

Guy Fawkes was an English conspirator in a seventeenth-century plot to blow up the English Houses of Parliament. Fawkes was arrested before he had time to set off the explosives. Some years later, Parliament declared November 5 a day of celebration for the failure of the Gunpowder Plot. These celebrations included parades, bonfires, and fireworks. It is a huge night in English culture when most parents take their children to a local community bonfire to not only watch a fireworks display, but help the children set off their own fireworks.

One November, after having been away from family for a while traveling, I promised my son Graham that I would spend all of the evening with him on November 5—first playing snooker with him at home and then taking him to Guy Fawkes Night, which was being held in a local park. Our other two children, Cameron and Heather, were away at Wheaton College in Illinois. After the evening meal, Graham and I played snooker. The phone rang, and Brenda answered it. She came into the room with the announcement that the call was for me. I was not willing to interrupt the game with Graham, so I asked Brenda to get details and relate that we would call back. The details were that a mother in Birmingham had a concern about her daughter, who had moved to Guildford and needed help. The daughter's address was in the congregational area overseen by John Selves, the elder.

When the snooker game was over, and as Graham and I were preparing to go to Guy Fawkes celebrations, I called John and shared the information with him. I then went with Graham and his fireworks to the bonfire event. There was no way I was going to break my word to Graham and get involved during the time I had promised him. We got to the Guy Fawkes celebrations, and after about half an hour, I saw Elder John with his son. I asked him about the situation for which I had called earlier. He said that the lady's daughter lived in a certain street that was overseen by a congregational pastor to whom he had passed on the need, and that pastor was dealing with the problem. The principle here is that neither pastoral staff nor elders were meant to be the sole ministers of pastoral care. Many more in the congregation can care for others if we affirm them and release them to their gifted ministries.

Not Needed

One evening service at Millmead, after a baptism, it was my turn to preach. The tradition was that baptismal candidates invited friends and family, and many of them showed up. My only involvement that night was to preach, so I sat with my family among the congregation, as was my usual habit, and simply delighted in the large number of people engaged in ministry. The evening congregation was large, with overflow videos beyond the main sanctuary. There was much music, celebration, and openness to the flow of spiritual gifts. Then came the baptisms. They were conducted by elders, house group leaders, and members of the house groups with which the baptismal candidates were associated.

There were eight people to be baptized. What I didn't know was that during the week, a group of praying women had heard from God that as many as were baptized on this Sunday night, the same number would respond to an invitation to follow Jesus. No one told me (they didn't need to). The service was powerful, and lives were so blessed by the testimonies at the baptisms that I knew my preaching would be superfluous. There had been so many vibrant "sermons" already. In due time I went to the podium and read Acts 16 and was prompted to invite folk who wanted to follow Jesus or recommit to him to come forward; eight people did. Here was community at work.

Because so many had been trained to give spiritual counsel after services, I was not involved that night in the ministry to those who came forward for counsel or healing. The story was not over. The practice of the church was to have the baptismal candidates go to rooms in the building with their house group leaders, elders, and family and friends for a prayer and sharing to end the evening. I left the sanctuary, as ministry was happening all over the place. I wanted to visit the rooms where those who had been baptized were, to see if I could help. I knocked at each door quietly and asked each elder or leader if I could help. Lovingly I was told, "No." I should have known; they were gifted and didn't need my help. The situation did not need an "official" or a "clergyperson." With deep joy for a wonderful evening, a congregation, and leaders who understood and lived a New Testament community, I turned to Brenda, somewhat choked up, and said, "Let's go home now. God is at work here. This is the church as it is meant to be."

Failure

When finishing my doctorate, I took a brief sabbatical leave to complete my work in the United States. I was still part of the leadership at Millmead. While in the United States, I was invited to preach at a somewhat unique church in the Chicago area. It had a promising future despite some deep leadership problems in the past. I won't identify the church further, for I have no wish to denigrate it. They were in the throes of completing a magnificent building, and they were in a search for a new senior pastor. To cut a long story short, months later they sent someone to England to suss out if I would accept the position of senior pastor. Two of our children had recently moved to the United States, and the third was planning on such a move, all to further their education. Perhaps I missed them too much, or perhaps I was going through a midlife struggle; I am not sure, but I accepted the call of the church and returned to the United States. The move was a disaster. I loved Millmead Church, and they loved me; there was no sound reason for me to leave. It was a disaster of my own making. I survived eighteen months in the Chicago-area church and resigned. I didn't steal church funds or run off with the secretary; rather the experience was simply a total mismatch. I had lacked discernment, but the greatest error was that I had failed to apply all the principles of accountability to Millmead Church that I had believed and taught. The irony was that in going to Millmead from Winnipeg, I had been open with the Trinity Baptist Church. I told them about the church's interest in me and wanted to know what they discerned God might be saying in the situation. I went for a three-week visit to the church. When I returned to Winnipeg, I shared openly with the congregation. We prayed together over a period of time, and there was no rush. With sadness, the church discerned that it was right for me to go. My family was given the warmest and most tender send-off by Trinity Church, but in this situation at Millmead, I had failed to discern the Spirit through the help of the elders. What hurts me still to this day was how blindly I had missed and neglected in my own life the very principles that made Millmead a great church.

I was now certainly in the wilderness. When it was obvious to both Brenda and me that I would soon resign the Chicago-area church, I was in a dark place in my soul. I wasn't leaving because I had done some moral failure or taught some heresy; I just didn't fit. Brenda, whose discernment and loyalty helped keep me from falling apart, gave me a copy of Henri Nouwen's book *In the Name of Jesus: Reflections on Christian Leadership*. This short book was life transforming to me and the beginning of a new journey. Nouwen uses two stories from the Gospels: the story of Jesus' temptation in the desert, and the story of Peter's call to be a shepherd.[4] Nouwen guides the leader from seeking relevance to prayer, from popularity to ministry, and from leading to being led. He challenges us to put aside our desire to be powerful and to stand simply in our unadorned, vulnerable selves, open to giving and receiving love.[5]

Brenda and I took time out for a few months and traveled to Fiji and New Zealand to recuperate. The lessons I was processing after this sad saga would take a long time to distill in my life, but bit by bit, they did.

Listening

New Hope Church in Victoria was my last ministry as pastoral leader before, eventually in retirement, I spent time mentoring at Southside Community Church where my son Cameron was pastoral leader. In the last few years, I served as a consultant to various churches in Canada and the UK that were going through difficulties. While at New Hope Church, I was also adjunct professor at Regent College in Vancouver. I ministered to the students out of brokenness and new understandings of leadership.

I had agreed to go to New Hope Church on the basis that after a couple of years, I would begin to present my conviction that leadership was both male and female in all areas of ministry. That was agreed. The early years were good times of establishing house groups, creative worship, and exciting outreach. During that time, we added to the staff both Paul Vermes, in youth ministry, and Shelley Schneider as associate pastor, both were in their mid-twenties and dynamic people. Shelley took over the leadership of the house groups. One day in that position, she taught me a further lesson regarding my own leadership. She asked to meet with me about the house group ministry. I listened to her struggles. When she had shared her

4. Matt 4:1–11; John 21:15–19.
5. Nouwen, *In the Name*.

thoughts, I somewhat (typically male) began to give her feedback from my years leading home group ministries and writing manuals on the same. I was in "fix-it mode." At some point, she stopped me. Despite my lectures on dialogue, I may have listened to her, but I had not heard her. Her response was basically that she had not come for advice but for understanding and support in her struggles. I should have known better. Soon I was to begin the process of affirming women in leadership. I needed to learn more about the different mindsets of male versus female on several issues. This was probably not the last lesson of my life ministry, but it was a valuable reminder of the control issues with which so many male leaders struggle.

Around the two-year mark, I presented a plan to the elders for addressing the issue of leadership. We shared that plan with the home groups, and by consensus it was agreed that I would teach for several weeks about leadership, dealing with the difficult passages on the subject and juxtaposing the *complementarian* views alongside the *egalitarian* views. Since discussing the basic teaching of the sermon was the norm in weekly house groups, we planned that for several weeks they should discuss what I had preached about leadership in my series. We then met as a whole church. There were two rules to be followed. First, anyone was free to share what they believed about women in leadership, and secondly, no view was to be debated or disputed. After that general meeting, we committed as a church to spend the next month in prayer about the issue. The final act was another church meeting where we simply took a vote. It is interesting that gender was not mentioned in the proposition on which we voted. In essence, it called for an affirmative or negative vote on the issue that *all leadership ministries in the church were open to those whom the church recognized as gifted and called.* It passed 93 percent in favor. I sat at a prayer breakfast a few days later with one of the respected women of the church. She told me that she had voted no because that was her conviction but that after the vote, she had decided to fully support the church in its decision because she loved her community of believers.

New Hope Church saw numerous conversions and growth in understanding of the ministry of the Holy Spirit. Like Trinity Baptist in Winnipeg, the people thrived in their walk with God as they experienced the truth of 1 Cor 12 and the importance of their own giftedness.

These stories could be endless, so I turn to brief statements about my personal joy of spending hours with some who I encouraged to preach or teach, sitting down in Bible study to help them prepare for their assignment on a forthcoming Sunday or midweek group. As well as that joy, there was more in working with elders and others when doing several weeks of sessions on how to counsel and do various other ministries. Hearing people affirm someone whom one has helped serve others is a greater joy than receiving the plaudits for one's own ministry. The stories above were meant to show from my experiences that the task of a leader is not to create a system that governs but one that empowers. Functional leadership is about making others able to share ministry and to equip them for service.

INSIGHTS

In what follows below, there are more stories as I explain more of my own strengths, failures, and struggles in leadership and the lessons that I learned thereby.

Raison d'Être

In a booklet prepared for the 2004 Forum for World Evangelization, C. René Padilla writes, "A New Testament perspective provides no basis for a hierarchical institution in which a small elite holds a monopoly of gifts and ministries, leaving the majority to limit themselves to 'submitting' to their leaders. . . . Integral mission demands the recovery of the priesthood of all believers to the extent that the Church become a community in which all members, equally, encourage each other to discover and develop their spiritual gifts and ministries in those countless areas of human existence which need transformation by the power of the gospel."[6]

The New Testament mindset about leadership flows out of an understanding that the church is a body composed of the priesthood of all believers. Paul reminds us that every church community has the resources to carry out its mission. Leaders are to discern God's gifts in others, and then stir them to love and good works.[7] I affirm this, and yet a caveat that has nagged at me often over the years is that in most teaching about leadership, the tone and emphasis seems to have been predominantly on "clergy" leadership qualities; giftedness for all is often forgotten by this mentality. The

---

6. Padilla, as quoted in Issue Group, "Local Church," §2.16.
7. 1 Cor 12; Eph 4:11–16.

Leadership and Character

Bible is full of examples of the fact that there are characteristics required by all God's people, who may have different spheres of leadership.[8]

This thinking which I present can be a challenge that raises questions by leaders of churches. Here are just a few of the issues and questions that I gleaned from my brother Alan's interaction with several leaders over the last couple of years. The questions arose out of pastoral leaders interacting with one another about leadership in the changing church and culture.

- How do we, as leaders, come to sense what the Spirit is saying and doing? How do we discern the agency of God, the actual work of Spirit on the ground where we live and lead?
- How does a leader begin to model something different for his/her community?
- What kind of leadership do we now need, and how does a leader invite the congregation to embrace the reality that much has changed and the pastor is no longer the expert with the solutions?
- As a leader it is too easy to be caught up in my own structures that get imposed upon everything. What might be involved in becoming a leader that can lay down this drive to impose my own structures and answers in order to attend and listen to what is happening beyond my picture of the world?
- How do we refocus our leadership work and our church perspectives from individuals to community?
- How do we raise up people from within the congregation and affirm the potential we see in them? How do we allow ourselves to get out from under structures?
- How do you convey excitement to the congregation and invite them into an experiment with you? How do you do this without suggesting the past is bad?

I note later on, under "Points to Ponder" in the section titled "Camaraderie," the importance of experiencing relationships with other leaders that can help one another work through possible answers to these questions about leadership.

---

8. Jesus spoke about this in Luke 22:25–27.

Character

The most important issue in leading others is character. Let me be quick to note that most believers are in some form of leadership, particularly parents at home, and therefore character matters for all of us. As I noted in the introduction to this chapter, there is a connection between leadership, personality, and character. We are somewhat blessed with, or stuck with, our personalities, which are so varied in all human relationships. We all have different traits, such as being outgoing, shy, upbeat, thoughtful, quiet, impetuous, funny, etc. God can use introverts and extroverts equally, as Jesus did with his disciples. In instances I have just listed, personality may not matter much, but there may also be a darker side of personality connected with psychological struggles such as compulsivity, narcissism, passive aggression, or other sometimes damaging behavior. Spiritual and professional counselling can be a huge help in some of these struggles, if they are pronounced.

"Character is an expression of an individual's steady moral qualities. The concept of character can express a variety of attributes including the presence or lack of virtues such as empathy, courage, fortitude, honesty, and loyalty, or of good behaviors or habits."[9]

Sally Morgenthaler shares this about character. She notes that her Swedish grandfather had a saying: "You don't know a man until you've had dealings with him."[10] This sentiment is reiterated by the Scriptures: "By their fruit you will recognize them" (Matt 7:16–20).

In N. T. Wright's *After You Believe: Why Christian Character Matters*, he expresses Matt 6:33 in terms of virtue and character, noting that we need to recapture the New Testament's vision of a genuinely *good* human life as a life of character. Learning can be a long process, as Wright indicates in his book. He states that it is like training to be an athlete. It is a deliberate process to achieve an alternate set of values that lead to righteousness.[11] Dallas Willard, in *Renovation of the Heart*, states that when we want to seek the kingdom and develop character, we need to have vision followed by intention and then the means of getting there.[12]

---

9. Wikipedia, "Moral Character."
10. Morgenthaler, *Worship Evangelism*, 57.
11. Wright, *After You Believe*, ch. 4.
12. Willard, *Renovation of the Heart*, 85–91.

A vital part of that character mindset appears in the video of Matt Canliss named *Godspeed: The Pace of Being Known*.[13] Appearing in the video with Canliss are Eugene Petersen and N. T. Wright, his mentors. Canliss learns in a remarkable way to live at God's pace of life in a Scottish parish, before returning after fifteen years to his present ministry in Washington state. One cannot miss in the video that the emphasis for leadership is on people, not on programs or innovative projects.

The Bible expresses character in spiritual terms. It is part of the spiritual journey on which we embark as we seek first the kingdom of God and his righteousness. Culture and nurture have something to do with the formation of character, but also character is formed by the choices we make in life.[14]

Running on Empty

Unless we deal with character issues, as well as come to grips with our time and what drives us, we will run on empty in our ministry. When I first moved to Winnipeg, someone told me about the winters and advised me to always keep the top half of the gas tank filled and not run on empty, lest I got stuck out in the middle of nowhere. Being male of course, I thought that I needed no maps, and I always ran on empty, until one day it happened—twenty kilometers outside of the city at thirty degrees below zero. The cold taught me its own lesson about running on empty.

Here are a few signs that indicate when we are running on empty in any form of leadership:

- We perform ministry without heart.
- We have oratory without power.
- We contend for doctrine without love.
- We engage in projects ahead of relating to people.
- We go through the motions of ministry.
- We look for quick fixes to problems and goal setting.

13. Lund, *Godspeed*.
14. In his book *Return on Character*, Fred Kiel defined a leader of good character as someone who scored high on integrity, responsibility, compassion, and forgiveness. Good *character* builds trust, and without trust people will not follow you. Without followers, obviously, one cannot lead.

- We cannot put adversity in perspective.
- We are driven and overworked. Drivenness is the expression of an insecure or proud heart.

It is here that I should insert my own experiences about personality and character weakness. Parker Palmer, in "Leading from Within", writes about the inner struggles of leaders: "The first shadow-casting monster is insecurity about identity and worth."[15] For a long time that was my issue, and it contributed to the times in my early ministry that I moved often and was part of the unnecessary move away from Millmead Church. Inside me was this upsetting voice that said the grass was greener on the other side. We all know where that takes us. Sadly, it can affect so many people, not only congregations, who may feel bereft, but more importantly one's own family, whose lives can be upended.

I genuinely wanted to seek first his kingdom and his righteousness in my ministry, but like Canliss in *Godspeed*, I was also driven and needed to be shaken. I share again here what I did in chapter 4 about living truthfully. I was raised in almost inner-city Liverpool; I learned certain values about how to survive. Prevarication, expediency, little white lies, and disregard for rules were part of the culture in which I lived. I was the Artful Dodger character of Dicken's novel *Oliver Twist*.[16] When I became a believer, I had a hard struggle to grow out of such things and grow into biblical values. A significant transformation from my own conversion was not just the elimination of certain sins but the espousing of truthfulness. That took a long time, despite the sincerity of my spiritual life, witness, and leadership.

There is a potpourri of leadership issues that come from or are dictated by personality and character. As with all of us, I was affected by them in my leadership, both positively and negatively. On the positive side, I was fun-loving, humorous, optimistic (the glass was half full not half empty), creative, responsible, merciful, and fair-minded. I was hardworking, rising very early in the morning to study or to do a project, but also I had the habit regularly to take time out to walk in the woods and talk to God or write poetry or just be philosophical about life. My Sunday sermons were nearly always completed by Friday noon mostly, my day off was Saturday, in order that I could be with my children, rather than Monday when they were at school. I was outgoing and had a heart for sharing my faith. I did

---

15. Palmer, "Leading from Within," 86.
16. Dickens, *Oliver Twist*.

not put on airs and graces but was a transparent, normal person. My love for Christ was genuine, and I spent time alone with him often, not always in formal prayer but, as I noted, in walking in the woods, along beaches, or hiking on trails, while reflecting on Scripture and singing hymns; those were the times I prayed for others too. For many years in my ministry, I had a flow of time commitment to the Lord that was daily, in devotions for about an hour; weekly, in the form of going to a retreat center for the day; monthly, in extending my weekly retreat to two days; and annually, when I would go camping for about a week in late August to prepare spiritually for the coming church year.

There was also a negative side to my leadership habits that I have shared above. Alas, for a long time I wanted to be well thought of and approved of. I sought applause and affirmation. A weak ego gave way to egotism. John Bradford, a sixteenth-century Reformer, when passing a prison said, "There but for the grace of God go I."[17] Whatever weaknesses people face, I could join them in Bradford's dictum. I am all too aware that as part of the human race, I have sinned and come short of the glory of God (Rom 3:23). Henry Twells's hymn "At Even, Ere the Sun Was Set" is based on the story of Jesus healing Peter's mother-in-law.[18] We all need spiritual and emotional healing at some point in our lives. This verse from the hymn is a comfort in our frailties:

> And none, O Lord, have perfect rest,
> For none are wholly free from sin;
> And they who want to serve You best
> Are conscious most of wrong within.[19]

I still have myopia about my character weaknesses, but if my heart stays fixed on Matt 6:33 and I stand ready to be challenged and corrected about my shortcomings, then I can be more secure thereby. Neither in myself, or others, do I call for or expect perfection, but now in the final years of my life, I see more clearly the urgency of integrity in leadership.

---

17. Bradford, as quoted in Hood, *Vocation of the Preacher*, 51.
18. Twells, "At Even."
19. Twells, "At Even," verse 3.

Models

As part of my ministry, at times I would meet with well-known Christian leaders. Most readers today will not know them, as they were part of my generation. With some of those I met, I felt privileged and glad, but with others, I felt manipulated and sad. I have such dear memories of the former group who, not because of their stature in the church but because their character, challenged and encouraged me in my own leadership. I have noted David Watson of York in chapter 5; space forbids me from sharing many more, but in that limitation, I feel sadness because they were such gracious people. I list just two others.

Dr. Paul Toaspern was a Lutheran scholar and pastor. When the Berlin wall was being erected to keep East Berliners from escaping to the west, and thousands were fleeing before the border was closed, Paul took his young family into East Berlin and set up a Lutheran mission to care for believers and disciple those living under Communist tyranny. Decades later, as I have noted in chapter 5, I arrived with a group of leaders from England (about eight of us) who had gained permission to see Paul. We met up with many Christian leaders from all over Eastern Europe who had also traveled to Berlin in order to discuss their participation in a conference in Birmingham, UK, called Acts 86. We made our way through the Brandenburg Gate checkpoint and walked into East Berlin in separate small groups, so as not to attract attention. We arrived at the mission and school that Paul had established. We spent the day with him and with those leaders in worship and consultation about the upcoming conference (which took place in 1986 at the Birmingham National Conference Centre, with over three thousand believers from all over Europe).

Nighttime came, and so Paul's group offered to drive us back to the Brandenburg Gate checkpoint. Paul and I drove together in a decrepit Lada, a Russian car he had waited ten years to get. I asked him if his children were at university. He said they were not because they refused to become Communists, which was a requirement for admission. He had formed his own school to train young Christians, and they were attending. I asked him about his parents. He had not seen them in twenty-five years because he was not allowed to return at any time to West Berlin. As they were old and lay dying, he had regularly gone to the Berlin Wall and shouted over it to the elders of his parents' church to learn of their health, until they eventually died. I hugged him farewell. (He was not allowed to go to the Acts 86 conference, but he got scores of European key leaders to go.) I traveled back to my hotel in West Berlin and threw myself on my bed in tears. I had met someone who understood Phil 3:10–11: "I want to know Christ—yes, to know the power of his resurrection and participation in his sufferings, becoming like him in his death, and so, somehow, attaining to the resurrection from the dead." The things that can drive us (as they once did Saul of Tarsus), such as popularity, position, possessions, power, etc., held no value to the Paul who wrote the Epistle (nor to Paul Toaspern). He had lost his freedom and his status as a respected Roman citizen and a staunch Jewish scholar, but he had gained Christ. Paul Toaspern had lost his parents, his career, his standing in the academic world, and a middle-class way of life, but he had gained so much that was more important.

Dr. Alan Redpath was an English Baptist biblical expositor of renown. He was a prolific author of Christian books. His early years of ministry were with Young Life in the UK. He pastored three leading churches, first of all Duke Street Baptist Church, London, and then Moody Memorial Church, Chicago (where I first connected with his ministry). In the mid-1960s, he assumed the leadership at the famous Scottish Baptist church Charlotte Chapel in Edinburgh. After illness, he resigned Charlotte Chapel, and his final ministry years were with the Capernwray Fellowship movement, which is now worldwide. It was during this final period in the early 1980s that he and I, among others, were to speak at the annual Filey Bible Conference and Renewal Week in England. I spoke one morning at the conference. Just before lunch, Alan Redpath came to speak to me. He seemed disturbed. He said something like this: "This won't do. You must take my place this afternoon. You are addressing the future; people must hear you again." After lunch he went to the lectern and, after a few words of description, said to the audience that he wanted me in his place to continue what I had started that morning. Until I hit my failure at the Midwest church in the United States, I would not have had the grace or character to do what Alan Redpath did.

POINTS TO PONDER

I do not know which leadership theory or style is best. Perhaps the old English idiomatic phrase "different courses for different horses" may fit here.[20] Leadership is not just about skills, expertise, and position of authority; it is about helping God's people to seek first the kingdom and to discern where

20. Oxford Reference, "Horses for Courses."

God is present in the local neighborhood or one's sphere of influence. Leadership and ministry are about experiencing and relating the glory of God ahead of *means* and *methods*.

Styles

The varieties of church forms currently shaping the styles of many churches of North America are more so extensions of our culture than principles derived from Scripture. One example of this concerns the leadership models that are often impressed upon us, as we are told to follow them if we are to succeed. The majesty of God and the mystery of our faith, as well as the righteousness of God and the beauty of his community, must be the quickening principles of the Christian life together in this fragmented culture. True Christian leadership shows that God is the primary agent—not business or psychological theories. It is easy in leadership to buy into professional mode. We want church success for good reasons, and so we try hard to achieve it by seeking to be leaders within systems or traditions. The danger is that leaders become professionals trained to manage and control the systems and, by technical expertise, to try to determine the outcomes.[21]

Parker Palmer agrees. He writes, in "Leading from Within," about Christian leaders whose mindsets are "functional atheism," the belief that ultimate responsibility for everything rests with them.[22] This is the unconscious, unexamined conviction that if anything decent is going to happen here, we, the leaders, are the ones who must make it happen. We must stop practicing leadership from a place of power. I believe the wisest approach is to use one's time in leadership to create a team that asks these questions: What kind of *people* do we want to deploy in the world? What kind of *church* produces those kinds of people? What kind of *leadership* produces that kind of church?

An old folk story says that over a gateway for those leaving St. Louis, Missouri, during the California gold rush, there was a sign for the wagoners that said, "Choose your rut carefully; you will be in it for a long time." The idea of a gardener is my understanding of scriptural leadership. I am, by hobby, a gardener and work carefully at nurturing different plants, knowing

---

21. Mark Branson and Alan Roxburgh, in *Leadership, God's Agency, and Disruptions*, write about "Modernity's Wager" as being the mindset that life can be lived well, without God.

22. Palmer, "Leading from Within," 88–89.

when to plant, prune, and fertilize. All plants need special attention. There is not one method that fits all. The gardener model stands in contrast to the educational model of leadership. In the educational approach, the teacher/preacher is the expert, spending many hours preparing the study and perhaps preparing notes. There is usually an attempt at application, but very often members of the community are receivers of information rather than participants in the learning process. However, unless the learning is directed at life-change and accountability for application, the educational model can actually work against real learning.

Preaching

Just as I believe in leadership, so too I believe in preaching, which means presenting biblical truths as a means of encouraging and teaching among the church community. It is also one of the helpful means of giving leadership. Here again the challenge is to preach the Scriptures in a way that reaches the believers of today, not yesterday. During a series of lectures in Russia, I ate lunch with students who were taking a course on preaching from a video presentation. I was not the presenter. They were convinced that John McArthur of Grace Community Church in California had *the* prescription for correct preaching, which they insisted was the *only* method of preaching. I suggested to the students that they needed to realize that McArthur had developed a system from a system that could not be found either in Jesus or in the Scriptures. It was the product of rationalism and was not the only method that was culturally or spiritually effective today. I went on to explain that different cultures respond to different styles of preaching and that different listeners needs different presentations. The weakness of the typical church sermon is that it assumes one type of presentation suits all; it simply doesn't. I suggested kindly to them that McArthur was an excellent preacher in his particular cultural setting.

In chapter 5 of his book *The Great Giveaway*, David Fitch challenges the presuppositions of exegetical preaching in contemporary church life.[23] Fitch's challenge about expository preaching does not involve a retreat from scholarship; it is rather a recognition of the effective principles of communication, understanding, and learning in the Christian community. When I was in my twenties, I was aware that many Christians read the church page of the Saturday newspaper to find out where they could go hear the

23. Fitch, *Great Giveaway*, ch. 5.

best preachers the next day in a given church service. Such a habit assumed that individuals can benefit from hearing the Sunday sermon, take notes, and go home with what is needed to live the Christian life in their own world. I saw this as religious consumerism. God's people need more than an expert who each week dispenses to solo individuals; they need more a community that engages Scripture together. The Bible gives an important place to preaching. It takes diligent effort to guide people by speech into experiencing the word together. The best sermons find creative ways and means to do that. "Rethinking Preaching: Limitations and Alternatives for Transformational Learning" is another excellent reflection on preaching in the contemporary church, written by Brad Brisco of the Missional Church Network of Kansas City.[24]

We must be careful that in preaching we do not present ourselves as an expert who knows and dispenses truth to those who are absorbing information that can be forgotten by just after lunch on Sunday. In this culture, we should not try to give too much at one time. Much can keep until the next week; what's the rush? (We should heed this idiom: the mind can only take in what the seat can endure.[25]) I once preached at a conference in Lancashire, in England. Afterwards, a little old lady came up to me and said, "I like you lad!" (I was sixty.) "You stand up, speak up, and know when to shut up!" (Insert a smiley. I think it was the best compliment of my preaching I had ever received.) Pascal once wrote, "The present letter is a very long one, simply because I had no leisure to make it shorter."[26] I often think this applies to much preaching. It takes a lot of effort to produce an effective short sermon.

The Bible is of utmost importance to our lives. We need to help the community engage Scripture together. I am not suggesting that we give shallow talks. We must do justice to what God has said by diligent study and spiritual contemplation to the section of Scripture that we are addressing. However, our presentation needs to be a foundation for congregational involvement in some form. We can help people learn in community through exercises such as "Dwelling in the Word," which is a spiritual practice of reading and dwelling in the biblical text with an openness to be formed and transformed by the living word. It is a unique way of allowing God to speak to us both individually and corporately, and of listening deeply to God and

---

24. Brisco, "Rethinking Preaching."
25. EnglishClub, "Head Cannot Take In."
26. Pascal, *Provincial Letters*, 417.

to one another. There is not one approach to Scripture study any more than there is one way to preach. Dwelling in the word invites God's Spirit to touch each one deeply and to penetrate to the innermost being of our personal and communal lives. Another form that should be encouraged, and which can be as effective as listening to a sermon, is *Lectio Divina*. The basic principle of *Lectio Divina* is that Bible reading is a personal encounter with God. This goes against what has prevailed in our church for some centuries: the text was seen as containing a message—doctrinal or moral—and once we got the message, the text had achieved its purpose. In *Lectio Divina*, we love the text, linger over it, read it over and over, let it remain with us, and let it teach us. Another asset can be a weekly study guide or manual based on the Scripture passage of the week, on which the sermon is given. We eat meals each day from menus designed to give us balanced and healthy food; study guides are meant to have that purpose. They have been a significant source of biblical and spiritual education for many over the years.

Accountability

One means of accountability is what the Celts called *anam chara*. The following is adapted from a few sources.[27] *anam chara*, or "soul friend," is a combination of close friend, spiritual director, and mentor. The soul friend is a personal relationship rather than professional. The soul-friend relationship is not hierarchical; the persons involved primarily consider themselves as companions along the way. The soul-friend relationship involves accountability. This willingness to challenge one another and hear each other's confession (a huge lack in Protestant life) springs from the trust and affection of deep friendship rather than from an unequal relationship. True soul friends do not depend on each other alone but root their relationship in God. The soul friend is someone who seeks to discern with us where we are on our journey, what the Spirit is doing in our lives, and how God is leading us. A soul friend is not a soulmate, such as a spouse, and so a soul friend should be of the same gender. In today's world of Skype and Zoom, long distance *anam chara* relationships seem quite obtainable. I cringe when I hear leadership spoken of as if the church board was city hall, etc. Howard Snyder speaks strongly to this in *The Community of the King*. We are brothers and sisters in a holy community. We are part of a team that is to be open, transparent, and free to share our deepest struggles. We need

---

27. Esquilin and Bekker, "Leading"; McColman, "Spiritual Direction."

to love and trust one another and to be accountable to and supportive of each other, discerning together the mind of the Spirit.[28] I failed at Millmead by shying away from accountability, not by intent but by emotion. I should have trusted what I believed.

Camaraderie

I keep hearing stories of pastors suffering burnout or emotional stress that requires them to take a leave. One must know each story, and there cannot be an overall fix; however, I think that part of the problem is caused by traditional views of leadership that push pastors into artificial and needless concepts of who they need to be and what they ought to do. There is such a vital need for leaders in various towns to get with like-minded people on a regular basis to pray, share, learn, support, and find hope and encouragement together. Leaders need not be down on themselves; our self-image comes from our relationship to Christ. Jesus lived for three years with his disciples; he ended up calling them his friends. We should do no less, particularly among those with whom we share leadership in a local community/church.

I long for the day when included in such a grouping could be community elders, as there are among Indigenous peoples or as there were in the Druids of the Celtic era. They could meet beyond the local church in a group formed of those from a wider neighborhood. These are people who, because of age and experience, have garnered wisdom and discernment that can be of great value to leaders in a given community. Together, all can learn that there is life after failure, in the midst of discouragement. All leaders have ups and downs, good times and bad, but we can be changed by these things, as I learned from my numerous missteps along the journey. What happened in the past can help us understand what needs to be changed in the future, but it doesn't define or determine us. In such a setting, vision, longing, and ideas can be shared and tested. Such a gathering must not be a typical ministerial setting, but it will likely need a day each month to be together. It will be time well spent. There are presentations listed in the Appendix under "Leadership Help," at the end of chapter 2, that can encourage us about leadership through the formation of cohorts. Such networks are of immense value; they can help one interact and gain fresh insight and ongoing support. Those sessions do not offer pat answers

---

28. Snyder, *Community of the King*.

to deep problems nor are they quick fixes or formulas for success; rather they are helps on the journey together.

APPENDIX

Books

- Henri J. M. Nouwen, *In the Name of Jesus: Reflections on Christian Leadership*
- Andrew Root, *The Pastor in a Secular Age: Ministry to People Who No Longer Need a God*
- Parker J. Palmer, *Let Your Life Speak* (particularly chapter 5, "Leading from Within: Reflections on Spirituality and Leadership")
- John Dickson, *Humilitas: A Lost Key to Life, Love, and Leadership*
- N. T. Wright, *After You Believe: Why Christian Character Matters*

VIDEO

- *Godspeed: The Pace of Being Known*[29]

---

29. Can be found online at livegodspeed.org.

EPILOGUE

Into an Increasingly Troubled World

The Church is to tell the truth in a society that lives in illusion, grieve loss in a society that practices denial, express hope in a society that lives in despair.

—Walter Brueggemann[1]

I haven't attempted in this book to cover the waterfront on all the issues facing believers today, but rather I have sought to encourage us to seek first, and to live out, the kingdom from a place of spiritual renewal of faith in Jesus Christ. From that place, we join with others in living a community life which includes "church" in some form. We go on to live values that are shaped more by Scripture and less by culture. The fulfilling life of the kingdom helps us to glorify God in a variety of worship experiences. The King of the kingdom was a servant leader; we must be the same. My writing has tried to help us to be both fulfilled and effective in this present difficult age. I hope that what I have shared in these six chapters will guide us on the way to seeking first the kingdom of God and his righteousness in our lives. Such action will help us cope and live fruitfully in the difficult years that surely lie ahead.

We humans see through a glass darkly, so in our narrow view of things, we may not understand how God is at work in the big picture. There is no need for either Pollyannaism or pessimism on our part, but rather we need

---

1. Barger, "Rev Walter Brueggemann."

Epilogue: Into an Increasingly Troubled World

belief in the *providence of God* in whatever circumstance or setting we find ourselves. It is *his* church, *his* gospel, *his* kingdom.

Relating to a fallen world happens in every generation. I don't assume that all this uncertainty is new. I don't have a crystal ball, but many signs seem to point to deeply disturbing issues that we have been already begun facing. The world is entering dramatic political and socioeconomic shifts. I was born in a time when the world was facing much trauma following a worldwide depression, which was immediately followed by the Second World War. I grew up during those war years. Life was turned upside down; my father was away for seven years in the army overseas, and as a child I never saw him or felt his touch. I spent many nights in bomb shelters, and with my mother and two sisters, we had only basics for food. I saw houses in the neighborhood destroyed each week. There was not much that was "normal" about my early years. The world order is changing dramatically, and the temptation for some in political life will be to gloss over evil forces so that they can gain power, in the hope of returning our culture to former days. That is not the way of God's kingdom. We need to be encouraged by Martin Niemöller and Dietrich Bonhoeffer, who at a Nazi rally in Germany, stood and declared that *Gott ist mein Führer* (God is my leader). They formed the underground church movement, the Confessing Church, in order to push back against the compromises that so many German Christians were making. The political upheaval in many Western cultures is very serious, and conditions will worsen. Christian leaders, particularly, must be like Bonhoeffer, be brave and push back against the all-too-common tendency to ignore the ways in which kingdom values are abandoned for the sake of political success or control.

By personality I am an optimist. My mindset is normally that the bottle is half full, not half empty. That disposition is fine for me, but I try to be sensitive to the different ways in which people hurt and struggle. God loves our fallen world and calls on us to care for it.[2] My view of Scripture looks beyond dystopian or nihilistic views of the future. The kingdom view tells us that it doesn't all end in a whimper or in darkness but with the trumpet sound and the new heaven and earth.[3] Speaking to the apostles in his final moments before Gethsemane, Jesus said, "In this world you will have trouble. But take heart! I have overcome the world" (John 16:33). His call was for us to stay in the world and be salt and light to the society in

---

2. 2 Cor 5:14–20.
3. 1 Thess 4:13–18.

which we live. What are we to do? How will we navigate? What is before and around us? N. T. Wright points out. The early Christians "did not think the world was getting better and better under its own steam—or even under the steady influence of God. They knew God had to do something fresh to put it to rights. But neither did they believe that the world was getting worse and worse and that their task was to escape it altogether."[4]

WHAT WE CAN DO

Believers should live in the world with distinctive mindsets that govern our lives based on Matt 6:33 about seeking first the kingdom of God. I suggest four that I have grown into over years of struggles and trial and error; they generally govern my life (albeit weakly at times). These mindsets, attitudes, or behaviors can help us to care for this troubled world. The reader may have his/her own set of important mindsets. These below are mine.

I think we are called to live *truthfully* (as people of integrity), *hopefully* (pointing the way), *compassionately* (feeling and enacting care and transformation), and *dialogically* (listening to one another with empathy and understanding). Each of these facets is really an extension of the dictum I chose for this book—to seek first the kingdom of God and his righteousness. In olden days, travelers were guided by the position of stars. If we keep our eyes on the star of Matt 6:33, we can work through these difficult life events. This is not done by human effort alone; this, too, is the work of the Holy Spirit.[5]

1. Live Truthfully (People of Integrity)

Truth has taken a battering in the last few decades. How we get information is changing dramatically. The seemingly regular news outlets of print, radio, or TV are losing their audience to multiple new sources of information. More and more of those outlets are being directed by just individuals with vast amounts of money and biased interests, opinions, and agendas (not that some traditional media outlets have not had their share of this in the past). A huge lack of trust in the media has developed, which is not always fair because there are many journalists who give their lives to trying

---

4. Wright, *Surprised by Hope*, 84.
5. Eph 1:15–21; 5:18.

Epilogue: Into an Increasingly Troubled World

to accurately and objectively present the truth. I am not sure one can appeal to the population to sift through sources of information to determine the accuracy or truth of the news they get, but it is vital that Christians do. We must prioritize the values of the kingdom in our lives and not the gaining of some form of power, be it political, social, racial, or economic, in order to discern the kind of information we receive. The families that try to live by kingdom values will have the best chance of their children and teens being objective about the information that barrages them daily.

When I speak of the loss of truth, I do not mean primarily the understanding of truth, as Pilate intended in his question "What is truth?" (John 18:38) or as Jesus when he said, "I am the way and the truth and the life" (John 14:6), but I mean simply the matter of not telling lies or making a deliberate distortion of facts or following social media's attempts to pass on false narratives and destructive theories. We now live in a culture of instant impulses mostly created by social media, which seems always to amplify extremes, as people react to minimal information and deny the process of research and discernment only to end up with shallow positions on almost everything that is on the Internet, to the distortion and destruction of truth.

John McCain, the late senator in the United States, wrote, "The phrase 'fake news' is being used by autocrats to silence reporters, undermine political opponents, stave off media scrutiny and mislead citizens."[6] We now are living in a post-truth world, one amplified by social media taking up the mantle of spreading the lies of politicians in numerous countries. We used to rely on facts to help us determine our actions, but what counts now is what we feel. Modern conceptions of individualism have caused people to believe that truth claims are only legitimate if I, the individual, agree. Conversely if I disagree, it must mean that whatever message was presented to me is not true. The governing social narrative is that truth is a matter of what one chooses to believe. That is a dangerous road to travel, and to an extent this mindset has been adopted by numerous social media outlets.

Truth matters immensely now, in a world were nothing seems to matter anymore and where traditional norms about law and justice are brushed away by the lies and subterfuge of politicians or popular sentiment engendered by social media, because we live now in a culture of inverted values; what was once wrong is now somehow rationalized into being right. We have a crisis of misinformation and disinformation in a world in which lying is now more often the norm in order to manipulate power. The great

---

6. McCain, "Mr. President."

deceptive rationalization that helps avoid being truthful is that we have gained "alternative facts." Conspiracy theories that can be sent around the world in seconds via social media destroy truth. Spreading disinformation using AI emboldens extremist groups, encourages distrust, and causes people to reject reliable sources of information. So many young people, especially, fear that they can no longer know who or what they can trust in today's social media presentations.

Truth involves how we deal with leaders and others who have consistently violated morality and trust or when they have manipulated God's word to satisfy their own appetites for power, position, or pleasure—and at the expense of vulnerable, easily silenced, and seemingly expendable people. The tobacco industry simply kept hidden the truth about smoking and cancer, and hundreds of thousands died. Fox News in the United States deliberately lied about the presidential election results to safeguard its income from sponsors.[7] The fallout polarized a nation.

Hannah Arendt, the German philosopher (1906–1975) who wrote *The Human Condition* and *The Origins of Totalitarianism*, had this to say about lying, in an interview with Roger Errera in 1974 (what turned out to be Arendt's last public interview): "If everybody always lies to you, the consequence is not that you believe the lies, but rather that nobody believes anything any longer, and a people that no longer can believe anything cannot make up its mind. It is deprived not only of its capacity to act but also of its capacity to think and to judge, and with such a people you can then do what you please."[8]

This is why I think that living truthfully is one of the most urgent of principles that cannot be compromised by Christians through rationalization or for any reason. Lies multiply, and thereby people lose faith in the truth and are increasingly susceptible to believe anything. Simon Shadowlight, in an article for Mile Hi Church published online March 1, 2021, entitled "Do You Have the Courage to Live Prophetic Spirituality?" writes that "to be a prophet in today's time . . . requires uncommon courage."[9] Simon quotes from Joan Chittister's book *The Time Is Now: A Call to Uncommon Courage* about this aspect of truth telling: "It is finding the courage to utter the first word of truth in public that takes all the strength we can muster. It

---

7. Bauder et al., "Fox."
8. Arendt, "From an Interview."
9. Shadowlight, "Do You Have the Courage."

Epilogue: Into an Increasingly Troubled World

is learning to say, quietly, unequivocally, I think differently about that, and then explain why."[10]

How deeply we need leaders in all levels of society and the church to be people of candor—that is, those who are open and honest, who by these qualities understand and express themselves sensitively and yet fearlessly, as Chittister points out. How important this is for believers in the political realm in these times.

We are called to bring the hope and light and the truth of Christ into the darkness that pervades our culture. If we remain silent when we should speak up, as Chittister calls us to do, then we are not living truthfully nor are we seeking first the kingdom of God and his righteousness.

Truth for Christians, in particular, and for the church, in general, is vital if we are to be believed and heard in society, but as I note above I am not writing about theological truth or dogma but about a lifestyle, for which the Bible has strong injunctions. God's people must insist in every area of our lives to be truthful, honest, trusted, and aboveboard, as well as to speak with integrity and fairness. We must take time to research facts as best we can before we hold opinions on anything, including politics.

It is in the Sermon on the Mount, just before his call in Matt 6:33, that Jesus said, "All you need to say is simply 'Yes' or 'No'" (Matt 5:37) so that there would be an integrity about our word and the commitments we make. We must be the people who would not change our word for personal gain. We are even willing to suffer if the commitments we make will cost us more than we realized at first.

I have been touched by the story of Cassidy Hutchinson, who testified to the January 6 committee in the United States. In her book *Enough*, she relates how Alexander Butterfield inspired her. Butterfield had testified against President Nixon fifty years earlier at great cost. Cassidy sought him out for advice, and among other things he asked her to go look in the mirror and to reflect on the person she wanted to live with the rest of her life. He told her that telling the truth would mean that she could always look in the mirror and be affirmed.[11] Christians can be a revolutionary people in many ways in our present world by telling the truth always and not manipulating facts to distort issues or diminish people. This may well be one of the most significant acts of witness to our faith.[12]

---

10. Chittister, *Time Is Now*, 63.
11. Hutchinson, *Enough*, 270–72, 329–32.
12. Dallas Willard writes, "The major cultural outlook today is that there is no objective

In the markets of Rome during Christ's day, artisans sold images and idols. There were two types on offer: those *without wax* (i.e., no blemishes that had been hidden by wax) or, indeed, substandard ones that were waxed over to hide faults. The Latin word for "without" is *sine*, and the word for "wax" is *cere*. From this comes our English word "sincere," which means free from pretense or deceit. A few years ago on a cruise ship tour with Brenda, we stopped at a certain port in Greece, and the usual tourist trinkets and souvenirs were on sale, I was intrigued by one stall that advertised its wares and watches in this way: "These are real fakes."

Christians join the culture's avoidance of truth at our peril. With social media now refusing to fact-check, there are many abandoning their services; however, some professionals and well-informed people are staying in them by creating special interest groups, thereby being alert to put factual information on record in refuting false or inaccurate messages. This is a salt and light alternative for Christians, regarding social media When we consistently act truthfully in the things about which I shared, we are expressing confidence in God's kingdom; we are living out Matt 6:33.

2. Live Hopefully (Pointing the Way)

By seeking first the kingdom of God, we do not face a future of despair but of hope that God will make everything new—including us. I do not want to cower or be made impotent by all the issues we face because God is sovereign, and as such this belief shapes my overall perspective of life. I do not have a laissez-faire attitude that keeps me from being passionate about things, but I am learning to look beyond them when possible and to look at all of life through the lens of God's kingdom. As people of truthfulness and what flows from that (such as integrity, fairness, and the righteousness of the kingdom), we live in a world that is in such great need of hope. A

---

truth or reality, that what we call 'facts' are only human products, that there is nothing more to knowledge than the 'best professional practice' as currently defined; in the words of Lily Tomlin, 'What is reality anyway? Nothin' but a collective hunch.' Moral principles, more than all else, are taken to be the mere prejudices of certain groups, none of which is superior to any others because, without God, we have no place to stand for perspective on the shifting scenes of human history, custom, and desire. The traditional view of truth has always been that truth, knowledge, and reality are not matters of what you or your group think; the task of truth is to come to correct terms with what is actually there, regardless of how you or others may view it. Truth is precious to human life in all its dimensions, because it alone allows us to come to terms with reality." *Allure of Gentleness*, loc. 18.

Epilogue: Into an Increasingly Troubled World

reporter once asked Lesslie Newbigin whether, as he looked to the future, he was optimistic or pessimistic. He replied, "I am neither an optimist nor a pessimist. Jesus Christ is risen from the dead!"[13] The answer is in the new and resurrected life given to us by our conversion. We are not part of the opposites of triumphalism or despair but of the hopefulness of having resurrected power to sustain us in whatever befalls us. For Christians, hope is not wishful thinking. Real hope lies at the heart of the Christian gospel. Through this we live in the meaning that life has given to us because we are Christ's, and his hope is within us. It doesn't mean that we don't have pain or failure or disappointment.

Many years ago, I was at a gathering at Holy Trinity Brompton Church, London, soon after the death of one of England's leaders—namely, Anglican evangelist and apologist David Watson of St. Michael le Belfrey in York, England. I was with several church leaders who were grieving this great loss. I had spent the previous year, during David's illness, standing in for him as team leader and speaker with the wonderfully creative team he had formed for his "missions" in the UK and North America. John Wimber, one of the early founders of the Vineyard Movement, had also spent time with David at the Yorba Linda Vineyard Church in California that previous year, ministering to him and praying for his healing. We were a saddened group of worshipers. After the service we talked about David and how his powerful ministry was so abruptly ended by his death to cancer. Someone asked why David had died when there had been so much prayer and ministry. The answer given by John Wimber was, "You win some and lose some." Despite my close association with both David and John at the time through various ministries, my response was that such a statement was dualism, and I disagreed. I said that God was sovereign and that he reigned, whatever the tragedy and mess that happens.

I think we can hope because our faith is not rooted in our emotional life, our pugnaciousness, or lack thereof, or our optimism, but it's rooted in the character of a God who has created this world and who has promised to renew all things and restore all things. Our hope is grounded in someone and something other than ourselves, and which is beyond our circumstances. Hope means that we don't curse the dark but light a candle—as Bono, the Irish singer and U2 leader, did during the Troubles in Northern Ireland. Through his witness, he went on to found the nonprofit

---

13. Newbigin, as quoted in Daniel, "Six Great Ends."

organization ONE Campaign, rescuing underdeveloped countries and helping the debt crisis in them.

There are many peoples, tribes, ethnic groups, and the like who have a history of troubles and subjugation (many still do). One of the great examples of living lives of hope is that of the African Americans in light of slavery, oppression, and Jim Crow. Eventually the civil rights movement with Martin Luther King Jr. was formed.[14]

Jürgen Moltmann writes much about hope in various ways in his book *Theology of Hope*. He indicates that, for the Christian, hope is the other side of faith.[15] His portrayal of the future is finding hope in a struggling world. N. T. Wright's *Surprised by Hope* encourages us in turbulent times to have hope based on the resurrection of Christ.[16]

For most of us, life is a finely woven combination of joy and pain.[17] A constant reading of the Psalms puts life in perspective. We are on earth for God's purpose under his sovereignty, experiencing now a resurrection life that will become part of God's ultimate plan for the redeemed. As believers our lives are blessed, guided, and cared for by our relationship to God in Christ. In the midst of the world's realities, which can be harsh and frightening, we are given hope not only to experience but to share with others by belonging to a dedicated community that lives with deep involvement

---

14. Howard Thurman writes about the Black African American and hope: "What greater tribute could be paid to religious faith in general and to their [slaves'] religious faith in particular than this: It taught a people how to ride high to life, to look squarely in the face of those facts that argue most dramatically against all hope and to use those facts as raw material out of which they fashioned a hope that the environment, with all its cruelty, could not crush." Thurman, *Life and Death*, 71.

15. Moltmann, *Theology of Hope*.

16. Wright, *Surprised by Hope*. This is about a fuller life in the now, not a "pie in the sky" future. His major theme is that we need to understand how the resurrection introduces us to the outlook that heaven is not about the big hotel in space but is part of the redemption of all things here on earth. With that in mind, we can face the painful issues of our day and offer hope. One day, as Rev 21 and 22 tell us, there will be a new heaven and a new earth; Eden will be restored. N. T. Wright states, "The ultimate future hope held out in the Christian gospel is for salvation, resurrection, eternal life, and the cluster of other things that go with them. Second, it is about the discovery of hope within the present world: about the practical ways in which hope can come alive for communities and individuals who for whatever reason may lack it. And it is about the ways in which embracing the first can and should generate and sustain the second. The early Christians believed that God was going to do for the whole cosmos what he had done for Jesus at Easter." Wright, *Surprised by Hope*, xi.

17. For Blake's specific interweaving of joy and woe, see Blake, "Auguries of Innocence," lines 65–69.

Epilogue: Into an Increasingly Troubled World

among neighbors. In such a community, we are reaching out to each other and beyond. When some may be in a dark place and feel hopeless, we can draw on the hope of those who know, love, and are committed to each other. We must become ever more sensitive to the reality that many in today's society have so little means of hope. They feel hopelessness and need our care by specific acts of compassion.

Psalm 33:13–22 sums up our lives lived in hope:

> From heaven the Lord looks down
>   and sees all mankind;
> from his dwelling place he watches
>   all who live on earth—
> he who forms the hearts of all,
>   who considers everything they do.
>
> No king is saved by the size of his army;
>   no warrior escapes by his great strength.
> A horse is a vain hope for deliverance;
>   despite all its great strength it cannot save.
> But the eyes of the Lord are on those who fear him,
>   on those whose hope is in his unfailing love,
> to deliver them from death
>   and keep them alive in famine.
>
> We wait in hope for the Lord;
>   he is our help and our shield.
> In him our hearts rejoice,
>   for we trust in his holy name.
> May your unfailing love be with us, Lord,
>   even as we put our hope in you.

In his book *Mere Christianity*, C. S. Lewis said, "If you read history, you will find that the Christians who did the most for the present world were just those who thought most of the next [world]." He said, "Aim at heaven and you get earth thrown in; aim at earth and you get neither."[18]

3. Live Compassionately (Care and Concern for Others)

To live compassionately means to take a negative situation and turn it around for good; it means to restore brokenness. It is to overcome evil with good.

---

18. Lewis, *Mere Christianity*, 134.

Again, it is in the Sermon on the Mount that Jesus explains this fundamental mindset of a true believer. To become a Christian is to be involved in the world that God has created; we cannot "build a sweet little nest somewhere in the West and let the rest of the world go by."[19] The old gospel song is simply not true when it intones that "this world is not my home, I'm just a passing through."[20] It is also important to note that the call of Christians in such a world is not to retreat into the ghettos of our cultural security, a habit learned from childhood for most of us. Perhaps the poorer district in which I lived growing up in Liverpool became almost a natural part of me. I felt that I belonged to the street and the area where I lived and was a part of its life. That stood me in good stead when I became a believer because this world was still my home, and I wasn't just passing through.

John Donne writes, "Any man's death diminishes me, / For I am involved in mankind. / Therefore, send not to know / For whom the bell tolls, / It tolls for thee."[21] The biblical truth is that we are our brother's keeper, contrary to Cain's lies about Abel. There are hundreds of NGOs and religious and secular groups that sacrifice so much to help the suffering. There is much redemptive and compassionate work going on in the world by Christians and non-Christians alike. We must be part of that action mindset.

Not only is God able to redeem and restore, but it is in his very nature to do so. Jesus is our greatest example of living compassionately. He said to Nicodemus, "For God did not send his Son into the world to condemn the world, but to save the world through him"(John 3:17). His main goal was to save the world and not to judge the world. God's desire to show mercy and forgive is much greater than his desire to judge because he is a God of mercy. In the same way, we can speak God's blessings and promises over our negative situations and relationships. We can stand up and be counted not as belligerent but as redeemers and models of an alternative life. How much did the clashes over the Covid-19 pandemic need this!

As believers who are called to live in the secular world, some have a special call and the ability to make changes or progress on a large scale, but all of us are called to live caring for people and trying to change wrongs within our unique circumstances and capacities. I have mentioned Bono in the UK, and I can add Tommy Douglas (Baptist pastor and then political party leader), who was voted the man of the century in Canada for his work

---

19. Ball and Brennan, "Let the Rest."
20. Brumley, "This World."
21. Donne, "Meditation XVII," 112.

Epilogue: Into an Increasingly Troubled World

in establishing the nation's universal health care system. Jimmy Carter died in December of 2024 at one hundred years of age. This American president and his wife, Roslyn, lived a humble life in Plains, Georgia, after his presidency and were actively involved in Habitat for Humanity, as well as other human needs organizations, until very old age meant that he could do that no more. There are hundreds more among the well-known and millions more among the unknown—ordinary folk and churches who live compassionately every day. They do a variety of volunteer ministries and give generously of their time, talent, and treasure for others.

The message given to Daniel was to seek the peace and prosperity of the city to which God had allowed the Jews to be exiled. We are to live in and care for our world and to love our neighbors as ourselves. There is no emphasis here on Christians recovering a lost culture/world that gave us privilege, position, and power, but rather that of discovering a new world under God and living in it. We are going to have to learn to be guests among our neighbors rather than hosts who have the upper hand and control. We must decide where real power lies (at the center of Christ's kingdom, not at the circumference in secular political gain). It should be the kingdom, and not politics, that defines us. We must live out such a belief in how we vote and how we get involved in different forms of political endeavors that seek consensus across the political divide. We must not be the ones that exacerbate political polarization. Although Western society is facing many terrible things, Christians will need to remain faithful to God's will and purpose by seeking first the kingdom of God in the coming decades.

In the introduction to his book *Faithful Presence*, David Fitch writes,

> Can the church reach out to the worlds around me in a way that doesn't judge them, alienate them, or ask them in some way to come to us? Can the church engage the hurting, the poor, and the broken with something more than just handouts? In this book I propose to answer these questions with the phrase, *faithful presence*. Faithful presence names the reality that God is present in the world and that He uses a people faithful to His presence to make Himself concrete and real amid the world's struggles and pain.[22]

I have a longtime Christian friend who is a psychiatrist with great discernment and insight. He used to travel periodically to a large church in the United States, one with whom I found little affinity. One day, I asked my friend why he traveled so far every other month or so to attend that

---

22. Fitch, *Faithful Presence*, 13; emphasis mine.

church, which at first glance didn't fit my friend's personality. His response affected me considerably. He said that as he went about the town in which the church was located, everyone spoke well of it and its care for the town. My heart was changed toward the church, regardless of whether I agreed with some of its expressions. This is what is needed more than all our church structures and sizes and forms of worship—namely, an authentic community of people who love God and their neighbors.

I am privy to a wonderful story of a Christian couple who shared Christian insights to officials of a closed regime by simply loving some of that nation's leaders. I cannot share more, but I am left very convinced that so much good happens beyond what we read and see in the press or the Internet's news. This is Scripture's everlasting call for us to both influence and care for the world in which we are placed, wherever that may be. The strong witness in the early church happened through how they lived out their faith and the fact that they had been with Jesus. I experienced this in Peru with my son Graham's ministry called Team Up.[23] They go among poor and struggling villages in different parts of the world, involving secular as well as religious groups to help children and youth through sport and to help families in such things as growing food for themselves. While I was there, one of the local Peruvian workers lost his house in a fire. The next day, scores of helpers started the process of restoring the house. Many groups around the world do this kind of thing all the time. I share the story to underline that the call on *all* of us is to live compassionately.

The ways and means of showing the heart of the gospel through compassionate living are legion. Some ways are obvious, such as helping with the homeless. Our involvement can be to support legislation that enables low-cost housing or facilities for the homeless, or by getting involved to care for those living on the street. Inflation and the spiraling costs of food leaves so many having to decide about paying rent or buying groceries. This should cause us to reflect and act on our frequent visits to restaurants that are now absurdly expensive. Special occasions are great moments in which to go out to a restaurant, but if we reduce our "special" times to eat out, then we can use the saved funds to contribute regularly to local food banks. Loneliness is one of the most serious of the modern social issues. Many churches and other social organizations work hard at meeting this need. We can do the same as individuals by coming to grips with what Jesus said about inviting people to a meal or a coffee or visiting them in prison.

---

23. See https://teamup.world for more information.

Epilogue: Into an Increasingly Troubled World

These are just a few kingdom acts that can help us to seek first the kingdom of God and his righteousness.

4. Live Dialogically (Listening to One Another with Empathy and Understanding)

Dialogue happens when people with different perspectives seek to understand one another. It means that they are not only sharing their different views, but they are also striving to achieve an understanding. Dialogue is at the heart of the incarnation (God's coming to earth in the form of Jesus Christ). It was the emphasis in the instructions Jesus gave to seventy-two of his disciples as they set out to share the kingdom message in various cities.[24] Note the dialogue in Isa 1:18: "'Come now, let us settle the matter,' says the Lord. 'Though your sins are like scarlet, they shall be as white as snow; though they are red as crimson, they shall be like wool.'" We need to learn the language of our contemporary culture by listening and caring sensitively; this is dialogue.

We cannot set aside proclaiming the good news, but now more than ever, we need a good dose of listening and discernment of the world in which we live and what God is doing all around us. We will have to swallow our superior attitude toward those not of faith and join them in their attempts to care for society, in their way as well as ours. We will need to swim against the tide at times and at other times go with the flow. We will need to celebrate good things in neighborhoods, whoever accomplishes them, but there will be moments when we will need to call out things that are wrong (dialogical living will best earn us the right to do this).

I recall the time I went to Samara in Russia (a large cosmopolitan town on the Volga and Samara Rivers that produced and launched the Soyuz rocket). I was invited by a local seminary and Bible college to teach for two weeks on comparative religions and cults. The era was soon after the breakdown of the Soviet Union, and there was an emerging atmosphere of new freedom.

I felt led to divide the course into two sections in light of the fact that for seventy years, Russian believers had lived under the clampdown on independent thinking. I believed that if I was to help the students deal with the many groups, religions, and cults that were pouring into Russia, I needed to teach them the nature of dialogue in the first week of class. I couldn't

---

24. Luke 10:1–17.

offer the students Russian books on the subject, so I relied on courses I had taken, books I had read, and the interaction among us as a class.

I taught that entire first week through an interpreter. As I ate meals and interacted with the students, I had to model that which I was teaching. It wasn't easy, so that was a challenge to me. At the end of the first week, a young woman student, who I deemed to be the most academic in the class, *let me have it* with a barrage of criticism in Russian, which I am sure the interpreter, also a woman, likely softened. The student was basically saying that the college had brought me to Samara to help them be skilled in telling the others how wrong they were. We didn't need the mumbo jumbo of the psychology I was sharing. In response, I simply said that I thought the incarnation of God was about dialogue. The rest of the class didn't agree with her. We went on to finish week two. The woman student warmed and mellowed during the second week, and the class presented me with a lovely colorful plaque in Russian, which they had all signed with a "thank you" on the back. I still treasure it and the memory of that fortnight with those Russian students, who were entering a new world they had never known before; this is a familiar experience for believers everywhere today.

This then is how we have to live in this world that has sought to gainsay Christian beliefs and marginalize us. Dialogue becomes a lifestyle and a vibrant form of witness, not as a method or a ploy but as means of respect for the other. To live incarnationally, as Jesus did on earth, is to be dialogical; it means to learn how to listen.[25]

During the several months that I was helping at a church plant, which met in a school for Sunday worship, it was necessary to have the school janitor always present. I noticed that he stood at the back of the gym while the worship went on. Each week I would say hello to him and listen to his background life and that of his family from Pakistan. Fortunately, I had been to Pakistan twice in various ministries, so there was some level of connection. One Sunday he showed particular interest and said his wife would like to talk with me, so I did to him what Jesus did to Zacchaeus—I invited

---

25. Len Hjalmarson, in chapter 5 of his book *Broken Futures*, writes about the importance of listening and discerning the culture in which we live by paying attention. In chapter 5, "Listening for the Future," Len writes about relationships, contextualization, paying attention through listening, and presence that leads to discernment (which he develops in chapter 6). Alan Roxburgh states in chapters 6 and 7 of *Joining God, Remaking Church, Changing the World* that listening and discerning should be one of the core practices in a Christian community: "Listening with our neighborhoods calls for congregations that practice listening with each other." *Joining God*, 85.

Epilogue: Into an Increasingly Troubled World

myself to his house for dinner. I had a great evening, ate food that I had not experienced before, and listened to the story of his wife's pilgrimage. She was an executive at a prestigious firm and was quite articulate on several subjects. Her ultimate questions were about the afterlife.

Dialogue for me that night was to share what our two religions had in common and then look at ways in which they differed, all the while affirming the importance of their interests and concerns. The evening was a beginning for her into an understanding of the resurrection.

Malcolm Muggeridge was, before his conversion to Christianity, the secular and agnostic editor of the famous British magazine *Punch*. In his book *Something Beautiful for God*, he tells the story of Mother Teresa and her work with the poor in Calcutta. Of his many meetings with Mother Teresa and those associated with her mission to the poor, he states that what overwhelmed him was the beautiful experience of being in her presence. He knew that he was the only focus of her conversation. She was fully present to him, as she was to all others.[26] Mother Teresa went beyond hearing to presence through listening. Hearing is part of listening, but listening is an active process that takes time and effort. Listening is difficult because it takes energy, whereas hearing is merely an involuntary response to sound. We see this in the well-known story of the boy Samuel, in the temple with Eli in 1 Sam 3. There are various organizations that can help us in this process of listening if we care to learn. Dialogue is a rare human skill; hence the reason that wars have existed in the world. It is through dialogue that people experience the miracle of personage and community. Dialogue is about successful communication, not just about telling people what they need to know. Dialogue is to love what blood is to the body. Arguments almost never reach people with the good news of our faith.

A dialogical person is an open person, willing to be vulnerable to others who may live in a different world. Such a person can listen with the heart as well as with the mind (both matter). He/she can learn from others as well as teach them. Such a person doesn't waste energy by being defensive but rather learns to give of self for the sake of the other. A dialogical person learns to live with the ambivalence that is so prevalent in the culture; the difficult issue of abortion is an example. Dialogue, and not political rhetoric, seems the most productive approach. Often the images we have of others, and they have of us, create barriers to communication.

---

26. Muggeridge, *Something Beautiful*, 45.

As I went among both Catholics and Protestants during the so-called "Troubles" in Northern Ireland and listened to them, I understood a huge barrier to communication between them was created by long-standing images they had conjured up of each other. When the Irish Republican Army bombed downtown Armagh, I was allowed in the next day to be among the community of people, both Catholic and Protestant, many of whom had lost loved ones. All were hurting in their souls. Their lives had been shattered. They were all seeking care, not retribution. I saw afresh that to live dialogically is to be incarnate to others as Jesus was to us.

Dialogue doesn't mean that we seek always to find a middle ground for everything or agree with everyone so as not to offend. I have not deliberately avoided facing the issue of dialogue over the different mores and changing attitudes to sexual topics in our society. It is a huge and complex issue that is dividing congregations as well as political factions almost everywhere. If some are failing at challenging one behavior, it doesn't invalidate one's conviction that another behavior may be wrong. It does mean that all perceived failing of biblical standards must be equally treated. My understanding of dialogue is that we must be open to the different views that we have of things and to the fact that sometimes, however hard we try, there may not be a solution that solves the problem. Usually this leads to severance of one kind or another. If we have acted dialogically, we maintain respect and care for each other even though we part.

Dialogue will help us to overcome barriers to communication on some very major issues. As believers we are often misrepresented in society because we believe differently in many cases. This can be mitigated, as it was for Daniel by the ways he dialogued and listened to others, so that when serious disagreements come, as they will, there can be respect, even by opposition or in the parting of ways. We are free to disagree but not to be disagreeable.

Four Principles

These four principles or attitudes outlined in the epilogue are somewhat akin to the life and teaching of groups such as the Quakers, or the role of the Mennonite Central Committee in its worldwide ministry of care. Dallas Willard, in his book *The Allure of Gentleness*, offers us the tone in which we should live in a world falling apart.[27] Such is true of many believers who

---

27. Willard, *Allure of Gentleness*.

Epilogue: Into an Increasingly Troubled World

sincerely seek the kingdom first. Such a mindset can be ours to live out with family, friends, strangers, the struggling, and all with whom we have contact and association. These four principles will not in and of themselves solve the huge issues we face or even make life easier in the tumult that is heading our way, but they will give us the hope and fulfillment about which I have tried to express in this book. Seeking the kingdom first is not an escape from reality, but it is God's way of believers both being fulfilled and effective. Kingdom life is not about being the biggest or the most powerful or popular, or about winning political battles over others, it is about a vision of life under the guidance and love of Jesus Christ.

Stan Biggs, who wrote the foreword to this book, contemplated all the recent shifts in politics around several countries of the world. He sent me an email that he had written just after the recent presidential election in the United States. In that email he asks the *quo vadis* ("Where are we heading?") and answers his question with these remarks.

"Live with gratitude, love the other, include everyone at the table, and listen to the only voice worthy of our attention, the Holy Spirit, who is a person, not an amorphous universal force, He offers this solution; Seek ye first the kingdom of God. My role? Live gratefully, love, and enter more deeply into a pursuit of kingdom realities. Our King is not headquartered in a nation's capital, rather, your heart and mine. We will thank ourselves for living in this reality rather than a reluctant concession to belief systems calcified in shallow dogmatic structures."[28]

The Years Ahead

Most who read what I have written will have numerous years left in which to go on *seeking first the kingdom of God and his righteousness*. I have tried to share that our pilgrimage is not a solo journey but one of community in some expression of church. I shared my excitement about Daniel and his three friends, who held a spiritual balance between living for their convictions and caring for the citizens of the different world in which they were placed.[29] While our fallen world is not something new, our care for its people must be new every day. On his death bed, William Bramwell Booth,

---

28. Stanley Biggs, email message to author, Nov. 10, 2024.
29. See Jer 29:1–14.

the founder of the Salvation Army, sent a one-word telegram to all those in the "Army." It read, "OTHERS."[30]

The life of a Christian is not simple or easy, nor does it fit into some preset mode, but I am convinced that Matt 6:33 can be a vital part of Christ's promise in John 10:10 that we shall have life in all its fullness. The old Welsh hymn "Here Is Love," which gained new popularity in the late 1900s, echoes my heart as I close this book:

> Let me all your love accepting,
> Love you, ever all my days;
> Let me seek your kingdom only
> And my life be to your praise.[31]

"Now to the King eternal, immortal, invisible, the only [wise] God, be honor and glory for ever and ever. Amen" (1 Tim 1:17).

APPENDIX

Further Insight About Facing the Future

I suggest the following books to read:

- The New Testament
- John C. Lennox, the Christian philosopher and mathematical scientist, wrote *Against the Flow: The Inspiration of Daniel in an Age of Relativism*. He has recently published *2084: Artificial Intelligence and the Future of Humanity*. This is a thoughtful insight into the future, which will be more and more driven by artificial intelligence. He outlines Christian responses in his usual brilliance, crafted in down-to-earth language
- *Reality, Grief, Hope: Three Urgent Prophetic Tasks*, by Walter Brueggemann, looks at the present state of the United States (but can apply to most of Western culture), and as Lennox does, he bases some of the present ills and future hope around the story of the Babylonian captivity of Israel
- Leonard Sweet wrote *Soul Tsunami*, looking at future church trends. He has followed it years later, along with Mark Chironna, in *Rings of*

---

30. Salvation Army, "About Us."
31. Rees, "Here Is Love," stanza 3.

Epilogue: Into an Increasingly Troubled World

Fire: Walking in Faith Through a Volcanic Future. In this book, they take a fresh look at the global megatrends affecting the church of the twenty-first and twenty-second centuries

- *21 Lessons for the 21st Century,* by Yuval Noah Harari, reveals the issues faced by humanity in today's troubled world

Discussion and Interaction

IN THIS SECTION OF exercises, there will be a quote from the book followed by questions for private reflection or group discussion and interaction. Choose one or more aspects of each topic as suits.

INTRODUCTION

- "Christ is teaching us how this new kingdom works. He draws a comparison between life in the kingdom and the life most live. He shows us there is a new reality available. No longer are we on our own, trying to navigate life in our own strength. Christ is urging us not only to seek the inner reality of the kingdom but also the practical outworking of the kingdom in our daily lives."

    What does it mean to you to seek first the kingdom of God (Matt 6:33)?

    What steps can you take to draw closer to this call from Christ, both in your daily life and the life of your church community?

- Discuss Les Biggs's statement: "The Kingdom of God has become an abstract concept disconnected from the past, disconnected from the dynamics of daily Christian life."[1]

- "Righteousness is, in part, about simple, practical, down-to-earth living for ordinary folk wanting to make God's kingdom their vision and way of life. . . .

---

1. Biggs, *Challenge of Understanding*, 19.

Discussion and Interaction

Experiencing righteousness in our personal devotional life is the ministry of God's Spirit. James Houston in *The Transforming Friendship* writes that the Holy Spirit is the friend who makes heaven real to us."[2]

Ephesians 5:18–20 and Luke 11:5–13 seem to show that the presence of the Holy Spirit in our daily lives is a matter faith not feeling. Discuss this.

CHAPTER 1

- "A vital part of living effectively as a Christian community is recovering the importance of a personal commitment to Christ and his influence and guidance in our everyday lives—at home, in our social life, and in our church ministries."
Discuss ways and means whereby this can happen.

- Everyone in the church needs a mindset that grasps that the Christian life is not just about church attendance. Instead, it is all about this truth expressed by [1 Pet 1:3–9]."

    Read and reflect on this beautiful passage, and share what it means to you.

- "We need to help each other participate in common activities where together we can live out our faith before others. This is our common task, not a specialized endeavor for a few."

    Discuss ways and means that you can accomplish this.

CHAPTER 2

- "I admired the men up the top of Arthur's Seat who were praying for the city with earnestness that morning, but they lacked the insight about what was going on in the city and knew not how to discern what God was up to in their rapidly changing community."

    How can we gain insight and understanding about the culture in which we live in order to be able to communicate the gospel in a meaningful way?

---

2. Houston, *Transforming Friendship*.

Discussion and Interaction

- "The church we have known since even the Reformation, does not represent "the" only way to express gospel and kingdom but rather "a" way."

  What fresh ways (that are consistent with Scripture) can shape the church today?

- We need to be communities of people who live out the kingdom in ways that cause others to ask what makes us tick. We do that in the context of our local neighborhoods where we are guests more than hosts. In what practical ways can this happen for your church?

CHAPTER 3

- "They are not of the world any more than I am of the world. My prayer is not that you take them out of the world but that you protect them from the evil one" (John 17:14–15).

  "Christians belong both to God's kingdom and to the world in which he has placed us. We need to be connected to and care for those who are in what colloquially is called the 'secular' world."

  What are some of the ways we can do that?

- "Seeking the kingdom and desiring to live righteously as part of the Christian life needs to be front and center in our dialogue with our culture, but we cannot do that unless we are lovingly and deeply involved in it."

  What are the tensions of living in both worlds/cultures, and how do we resolve them?

- "Interpreting [exegeting] Scripture in light of our contemporary culture is a challenging task, but the more vital task is to interpret and understand the culture in light of Scripture. . . . Our life in the kingdom is about pleasing God, not about pleasing ourselves or choosing self-actualization; it is more about choosing self-denial."

  How do we do wrestle with these issues in practical terms?

Discussion and Interaction

- "What Daniel and his friends offered was a willingness to serve the Babylonian culture well, while at the same time being resolved to stand up to it, as the fiery furnace in Dan 3 and the lion's den in Dan 6 clearly reveal. . . .

  . . . Culture shapes, controls, and determines our thinking far more than we realize. . . . The tension will always be how we hold conviction and compassion. . . .

  . . . We are called to speak out of a different cultural narrative than the secular world; one that is guided by Matt 6:33."

  Discuss ways in which we can do this effectively in our daily lives.

CHAPTER 4

- "To seek first the kingdom of God and his righteousness is not meant to be a lonely or individualistic journey. By design, in both Scripture and nature, we are meant to be part of a collective life, in a similar manner to how we mature as children in the context of family."

  "Community is a fluid and existential thing. Like love, it is a more observable than definable experience. Life together is more caught than taught, programmed, or planned."

  What have been your experiences in endeavoring to be part of some form of Christian community? What worked? What didn't?

- "Community can't be manufactured by human programming; it grows out of an understanding and desire related to Matt 6:33 and a commitment to each other. . . .

  Community needs to be born out of a heart's desire. It is lived with various people in various ways. Our life together is the fruit of people living authentically and lovingly with an expanding pool of growing friendships that defies age, interests, ethnicity, and societal status. It involves accountability, responsibility, proximity, and mission."

  Discuss ways in which you can gather with others to set out on such a journey OR help to make your small group more of a community than a meeting.

Discussion and Interaction

- Watch the movie *The Way* and discuss what you learned from it and what the implications are for your life together with others.
- How has this chapter of the book helped you to understand or experience community?

CHAPTER 5

- "Our goals in worship are:
    - to honor him
    - to respond to his love
    - to express our love to him
    - to bless him
    - to allow him to bless us
    - to affirm our faith
    - to hear the voice of God
    - to be motivated for service/ministry
    - to experience existentially his presence and power"

    Share ways in which each of these goals can be experienced in your life.

- "There are three fallacies we can make about public worship—namely, that it is about place, about form, or about us. In *Celebration of Discipline*, Richard Foster writes, 'Worship is the human response to the divine initiative. Singing, praying, praising all may lead to worship, but worship is more than any of them. Our spirit must be ignited by the divine fire. As a result, we need not be overly concerned with the question of a correct form for worship. The issue of high liturgy or low liturgy, this form or that form is peripheral rather than central.'"[3]

    Discuss Richard Foster's statement.

- "What grips me for today's church is not so much a particular form of . . . worship or the expression of any one generation, but the reality that there are basics to worship that flow through the centuries.

3. Foster, *Celebration of Discipline*, 197–98.

Discussion and Interaction

... It is those basics that count the most in any worship experience." What do you think are the basics of worship, and how can you experience them?

"What is really needed beyond a seeker sensitive emphasis is Spirit sensitive worship. We must be careful about studying what consumers want rather than what God does. . . .

Worship is not just about self-expression but about experiencing something transcendent. . . .

. . . It is God, not the seeker or even the Christian, who is the subject and object of our worship."

Discuss your reaction to what Isaiah experienced in Isa 6:1–9. How can that be part of your worship experience with others?

- "My longing is that we learn to recover or establish intergenerational worship that grows out of intergenerational community."

What do you think we need to do to include all generations in public worship?

CHAPTER 6

- "The task of a leader is not to create a system that governs but one that empowers. Functional leadership is about making others able to share ministry and to equip them for service."

What do you think is the lesson of the "Guy Fawkes" or "Not Needed" sections of this chapter for your leadership?

- The New Testament mindset about leadership flows out of an understanding that the church is a body composed of the priesthood of all believers. Paul reminds us that every church community has the resources to carry out its mission. Leaders are to discern God's gifts in others, and then stir them to love and good works. . . .

. . . Leadership and ministry are about experiencing and relating the glory of God ahead of means and methods."

What qualities do you think are needed to gain that kind of relationship among the people one serves?

Discussion and Interaction

- "I was now certainly in the wilderness. When it was obvious to both Brenda and me that I would soon resign the Chicago-area church, I was in a dark place in my soul. I wasn't leaving because I had done some moral failure or taught some heresy; I just didn't fit. Brenda, whose discernment and loyalty helped keep me from falling apart, gave me a copy of Henri Nouwen's book *In the Name of Jesus: Reflections on Christian Leadership*. This short book was life transforming to me and the beginning of a new journey."

  In whatever form of leadership you are involved, how has a particular failure shaped you? What did you learn? How have you recovered?

- "In a booklet prepared for the 2004 Forum for World Evangelization, C. René Padilla writes, 'A New Testament perspective provides no basis for a hierarchical institution in which a small elite holds a monopoly of gifts and ministries, leaving the majority to limit themselves to "submitting" to their leaders. . . . Integral mission demands the recovery of the priesthood of all believers to the extent that the Church become a community in which all members, equally, encourage each other to discover and develop their spiritual gifts and ministries in those countless areas of human existence which need transformation by the power of the gospel.'"[4]

  Assuming your pastoral leaders understand and want what is stated in the paragraph above, how do you, as one of the congregation, help and support the implementation of what Padilla writes?

- "The Bible expresses character in spiritual terms. It is part of the spiritual journey on which we embark as we seek first the kingdom of God and his righteousness. Culture and nurture have something to do with the formation of character, but also character is formed by the choices we make in life. . . .

  There is a potpourri of leadership issues that come from or are dictated by personality and character."

  Discuss the difference between personality and character, and determine for yourselves the importance of character in your life and leadership.

---

4. Padilla, as quoted in Issue Group, "Local Church," §2.16.

- "Leaders need not be down on themselves; our self-image comes from our relationship to Christ. Jesus lived for three years with his disciples; he ended up calling them his friends. We should do no less, particularly with those with whom we share leadership in a local community/church."

"They [leaders] could meet beyond the local church in a group formed of those from a wider neighborhood. . . . All leaders have ups and downs, good times and bad, but we can be changed by these things, as I learned from my numerous missteps along the journey. . . . In such a setting, vision, longing, and ideas can be shared and tested. Such a gathering must not be a typical ministerial setting, but it will likely need a day each month to be together. It will be time well spent."

What practical steps are needed for leaders in various categories of the Christian life to form support groups in their community?

EPILOGUE

- "Believers should live in the world with distinctive mindsets that govern our lives based on Matt 6:33 about seeking first the kingdom of God. . . . These mindsets, attitudes, or behaviors can help us to care for this troubled world."

"I think we are called to live *truthfully* (as people of integrity), *hopefully* (pointing the way), *compassionately* (feeling and enacting care and transformation), and *dialogically* (listening to one another with empathy and understanding)."

Over a period of several sessions, look at each of the four mindsets and discuss their relevance to you and how you might go about implementing them or deepening them in your life. Our perspective on things, including our political bias, is shaped not by Scripture but by our upbringing. We could make a to-do list of things involved in being compassionate to those in need.

Bibliography

Arendt, Hannah. "Hannah Arendt: From an Interview." Interview by Roger Errera. *New York Review of Books*, Oct. 26, 1978. https://www.nybooks.com/articles/1978/10/26/hannah-arendt-from-an-interview/.
———. *The Human Condition*. Chicago: University of Chicago Press, 1958.
———. *The Origins of Totalitarianism*. New York: Harcourt, Brace & World, 1951.
Auber, Harriet. "Our Blest Redeemer." In *CPWI Hymnal*, #291. Saint John, Barbados: Church in the Province of the West Indies, 2010. https://hymnary.org/text/our_blest_redeemer_ere_he_breathed.
Ball, Ernest R., and J. Keirn Brennan. "Let the Rest of the World Go By." 1919. Historic Sheet Music Collection, #832. https://digitalcommons.conncoll.edu/sheetmusic/832/.
Banco Sabadell. "Som Sabadell Flashmob—Banco Sabadell." May 31, 2012. Video, 5:40. https://www.youtube.com/watch?v=GBaHPND2QJg.
Banks, Robert. *Paul's Idea of Community*. Rev. ed. Grand Rapids: Baker Academic, 1994.
Bauder, David, et al. "Fox, Dominion Reach $787M Settlement over Election Claims." *Associated Press*, Apr. 18, 2023. https://apnews.com/article/fox-news-dominion-lawsuit-trial-trump-2020-0ac71f75acfacc52ea80b3e747fb0afe.
Bauman, Zygmunt. *Liquid Modernity*. Cambridge: Polity, 2000.
Barger, T. K. "Rev. Walter Brueggemann Draws Parallels from Today's Society to Ancient Times." *Toledo Blade*, Jan. 11, 2014. https://www.toledoblade.com/news/religion/2014/01/11/Ohio-author-strives-for-the-truth/stories/20140111004.
Biggs, Les. *The Challenge of Understanding the Kingdom of God*. PhD diss., Carey Theological College of Vancouver, May 2011.
Blake, William. "Auguries of Innocence." In *The Complete Poems*, edited by Alicia Ostriker, 492–95. London: Penguin, 1977.
Block, Peter. *Community: The Structure of Belonging*. San Francisco: Berrett-Koehler, 2008.
Bonar, Horatius. "I Heard the Voice of Jesus Say." In *Hymns and Devotions for Daily Worship*, #219. Louisville: Hymnology Archive, 2024. https://hymnary.org/text/i_heard_the_voice_of_jesus_say_come_unto.
Bonhoeffer, Dietrich. *Life Together: The Classic Exploration of Christian Community*. Translated by John W. Doberstein. New York: Harper & Row, 1954.
———. *The Cost of Discipleship*. New York: Touchstone, 1995.
Boyle, Danny, dir. *Yesterday*. Universal City, CA: Universal, 2019.
Branson, Mark Lau, and Alan J. Roxburgh. *Leadership, God's Agency, and Disruptions: Confronting Modernity's Wager*. Minneapolis: Fortress, 2021.

Bibliography

Brisco, Brad. "Rethinking Preaching: Limitations and Alternatives for Transformational Learning." Missional Church Network, Oct. 27, 2024. https://www.missionalchurchnetwork.com/blog/rethinking-preaching-limitations-and-alternatives-for-transformational-learning.

Brooks, Phillips. "O Little Town of Bethlehem." In *Psalms and Hymns to the Living God*, edited by Scott Aniol, #232. Douglasville, GA: G3 Ministries, 2023. https://hymnary.org/text/o_little_town_of_bethlehem.

Brueggemann, Walter. *Reality, Grief, Hope: Three Urgent Prophetic Tasks*. Grand Rapids: Eerdmans, 2014.

Brumley, Albert E. "This World Is Not My Home." In *Abiding Faith*, edited by R. E. Winsett, #121. Dayton, TN: Winsett, 1947.

Buchanan, Mark. *Your Church Is Too Safe: Why Following Christ Turns the World Upside Down*. Grand Rapids: Zondervan, 2012.

Chittister, Joan. *The Time Is Now: A Call to Uncommon Courage*. New York: Convergent, 2019.

Columbus, Chris, dir. *Harry Potter and the Sorcerer's Stone*. Burbank, CA: Warner Bros., 2001.

The Commons Network. "Who Are We?" https://www.thecommonscooperative.com/.

Cosby, Gordon. *Handbook for Mission Groups*. Washington, DC: Shalem Institute, 1997.

Crossroads Initiative. "Our Heart Is Restless Until It Rests in You: Augustine." July 1, 2021. https://www.crossroadsinitiative.com/media/articles/ourheartisrestlessuntilitrestsinyou/.

Crouch, Andy. *Culture Making: Recovering Our Creative Calling*. Downers Grove, IL: InterVarsity, 2008.

Daniel, Blake. "The Six Great Ends of the Church." First Presbyterian Church (blog), Apr. 12, 2021. https://www.sylvapres.org/fpc-blog/2021/4/12/the-six-great-ends-of-the-church.

Dickens, Charles. *Oliver Twist: Wordsworth Classic Series*. Ware, UK: Wordsworth Classics, 1992.

Dickson, John. *Humilitas: A Lost Key to Life, Love, and Leadership*. Grand Rapids: Zondervan, 2011.

Donne, John. "Meditation XVII." In *Devotions upon Emergent Occasions*, edited by Charles W. Eliot. New York: P. F. Collier & Son, 1909.

Driver, John. *The Kingdom of God: Goal of Messianic Mission*. Scottdale, PA: Herald, 1980.

Dulles, Avery. *Models of the Church*. Garden City, NY: Doubleday, 1974.

EnglishClub. "The Head Cannot Take In More than the Seat Can Endure." https://www.englishclub.com/ref/esl/Quotes/Language/The_head_cannot_take_in_more_than_the_seat_can_endure._2549.php.

Esquilin, Cynthia L., and Corné J. Bekker. "Leading as a Soul Friend: The Anamchara Model of Spiritual Direction." *Inner Resources for Leaders* 2.2 (2007) 1–10. https://www.regent.edu/acad/global/publications/innerresources/vol2iss2/esquilin_bekker.pdf.

Estevez, Emilio, dir. *The Way*. Santa Monica, CA: Icon Productions, 2010.

Fee, Gordon D. *Paul, the Spirit, and the People of God*. Grand Rapids: Baker Academic, 1996.

Fitch, David. *The Church of Us vs. Them: Freedom from a Faith That Feeds on Making Enemies*. Grand Rapids: Brazos, 2019.

Bibliography

———. *Faithful Presence: Seven Disciplines That Shape the Church for Mission*. Downers Grove, IL: InterVarsity, 2016.

———. *The Great Giveaway: Reclaiming the Mission of the Church from Big Business, Parachurch Organizations, Psychotherapy, Consumer Capitalism, and Other Modern Maladies*. Grand Rapids: Baker, 2005.

———. *What Is the Church and Why Does It Exist?* Grand Rapids: Baker Academic, 2021.

Fosner, Verlon. *Dinner Church: Building Bridges by Breaking Bread*. Nashville: Seedbed, 2014.

Foster, Richard. *Celebration of Discipline: The Path to Spiritual Growth*. London: Hodder & Stoughton, 1989.

Green, Michael. *I Believe in Satan's Downfall: The Reality of Evil and the Victory of Christ*. London: Hodder & Stoughton, 1981.

Halter, Hugh. *Righteous Brood: Making the Mission of God a Family Story*. Grand Rapids: Baker, 2014.

Harari, Yuval Noah. *21 Lessons for the 21st Century*. New York: Spiegel & Grau, 2018.

Harper, Michael. *A New Way of Living*. London: Hodder & Stoughton, 1973.

Hirsch, Alan. *The Forgotten Ways: Reactivating the Missional Church*. Grand Rapids: Brazos, 2013.

Hjalmarson, Len. *Broken Futures: Leaders and Churches Lost in Transition*. Skyforest, CA: Urban Loft, 2018.

Holy Trinity Brompton. "Our Story." https://www.htb.org/story.

Hood, Edwin Paxton. *The Vocation of the Preacher*. London: Hodder & Stoughton, 1881.

Houston, John. *The Transforming Friendship: A Guide to Prayer*. Colorado Springs, CO: Cook, 2007.

Hull, Eleanor H. "Be Thou My Vision." In *Hymns and Devotions for Daily Worship*, #268. Louisville: Hymnology Archive, 2024. https://hymnary.org/text/be_thou_my_vision_o_lord_of_my_heart.

Hutchinson, Cassidy. *Enough*. New York: Simon & Schuster, 2023.

Hybels, Bill, and Mark Mittelberg. *Becoming a Contagious Christian*. Grand Rapids: Zondervan, 1994.

Idiom Origins. "Cut One's Coat According to One's Cloth." https://idiomorigins.org/origin/cut-ones-coat-according-to-ones-cloth.

Issue Group. "The Local Church in Mission." *Lausanne Occasional Papers* 39 (2004). https://lausanne.org/occasional-paper/holistic-mission-lop-39.

Jewish Roots 101. "Church of the Redeemer Houston—First Century Church." Produced by Jim Becka. July 11, 2012. Video, 9:41. https://www.youtube.com/watch?v=GRC6lcPKI9o.

Johnson, Ben. "St Columba and the Isle of Iona." Historic UK. https://www.historic-uk.com/HistoryUK/HistoryofScotland/St-Columba-the-Isle-of-Iona/.

Keller, Timothy. *Center Church: Doing Balanced, Gospel-Centered Ministry in Your City*. Grand Rapids: Zondervan, 2012.

Kiel, Fred. *Return on Character: The Real Reason Leaders and Their Companies Win*. Brighton, MA: Harvard Business Review, 2015.

Kierkegaard, Søren. *Purity of Heart Is to Will One Thing*. Translated by Douglas V. Steere. Toronto, ON: HarperCollins Canada, 2011. Kindle.

Kraybill, Donald. *The Upside-Down Kingdom*. Anniversary ed. Harrisonburg, VA: Herald, 2018.

Bibliography

Kreider, Alan, and Eleanor Kreider. *Worship and Mission After Christendom*. Huntington, IN: Herald, 2011.

L'Arche International. *Charter of the Communities of L'Arche*. 1993. https://archive.larcheusa.org/wp-content/uploads/2011/03/Charter-of-LArche.pdf.

Lennox, John C. *Against the Flow: The Inspiration of Daniel in an Age of Relativism*. Oxford: Monarch, 2015.

———. *2084: Artificial Intelligence and the Future of Humanity*. Grand Rapids: Zondervan, 2020.

Lewis, C. S. *Mere Christianity*. New York: HarperOne, 1952.

———. *Surprised by Joy: The Shape of My Early Life*. London: Bles, 1955.

Lund, Danny, dir. *Godspeed: The Pace of Being Known*. Featuring Matt Canlis, Eugene Peterson, and N. T. Wright. Produced by The Ranch Studios, 2017. Video, 36:53. https://www.livegodspeed.org/watchgodspeed.

Maries, Andrew. *One Heart, One Voice: The Rich and Varied Resource of Music in Worship*. London: Hodder & Stoughton, 1985.

McCain, John. "Mr. President, Stop Attacking the Press." *Washington Post*, Jan. 16, 2018. https://www.washingtonpost.com/opinions/mr-president-stop-attacking-the-press/2018/01/16/9438c0ac-fafo-11e7-a46b-a3614530bd87_story.html.

McColman, Carl. "Spiritual Direction with Carl McColman." Anamchara. https://www.anamchara.com/spiritual-direction/.

McKnight, John, and Peter Block. *The Abundant Community: Awakening the Power of Families and Neighborhoods*. San Francisco: Berrett-Koehler, 2010.

McKnight, Scot. *Kingdom Conspiracy: Returning to the Radical Mission of the Local Church*. Grand Rapids: Brazos, 2014.

Metro Church. "Community Prayer and Benediction." About Metro Church. https://metrocommunity.ca/metrochurch.

Milton, John. "Sonnet 19: When I Consider How My Light Is Spent." Poetry Foundation, https://www.poetryfoundation.org/poems/44750/sonnet-19-when-i-consider-how-my-light-is-spent.

Moltmann, Jürgen. *Theology of Hope: On the Ground and the Implications of a Christian Eschatology*. Translated by James W. Leitch. New York: Harper & Row, 1967.

Morgenthaler, Sally. *Worship Evangelism: Inviting Unbelievers into the Presence of God*. Grand Rapids: Zondervan, 1995.

Muggeridge, Malcolm. *Something Beautiful for God*. San Francisco: HarperOne, 2003.

Mulder, John M., and Hugh Thomson Kerr, eds. *Finding God: A Treasury of Conversion Stories*. Grand Rapids: Eerdmans, 2012.

Murray, Stuart. *Church After Christendom*. Milton Keynes: Paternoster, 2004.

Newbigin, Lesslie. *Foolishness to the Greeks: The Gospel and Western Culture*. Grand Rapids: Eerdmans, 1986.

———. *The Gospel in a Pluralistic Society*. Grand Rapids: Eerdmans, 1989.

———. *The Household of God: Lectures on the Nature of Church*. London: SCM, 1953.

———. *The Open Secret: An Introduction to the Theology of Mission*. Grand Rapids: Eerdmans, 1978.

Niebuhr, H. Richard. *Christ and Culture*. New York: Harper & Row, 1951.

Nouwen, Henri J. M. *In the Name of Jesus: Reflections on Christian Leadership*. New York: Crossroad, 1989.

O'Connor, Elizabeth. *Call to Commitment: The Story of the Church of the Saviour, Washington, D.C.* New York: Harper & Row, 1963.

Bibliography

Oxford Reference. "Horses for Courses." Oxford University Press. https://www.oxfordreference.com/view/10.1093/acref/9780199539536.001.0001/acref-9780199539536-e-1095.

Palmer, Parker J. "Leading from Within." In *Let Your Life Speak: Listening for the Voice of Vocation*, 73–94. San Francisco: Jossey-Bass, 2000.

———. *A Place Called Community*. Wallingford, PA: Pendle Hill, 1978.

Pascal, Blaise. *The Provincial Letters*. Edited by O. W. Wight. New York: Hurd & Houghton 1866. https://www.loc.gov/resource/gdcmassbookdig.provincialletter01pasc/?st=gallery.

Peck, M. Scott. *The Different Drum: Community Making and Peace*. New York: Simon & Schuster, 1987.

Rees, William. "Here Is Love." Translated by William Edwards. In *Psalms and Hymns to the Living God*, edited by Scott Aniol, #315. Douglasville, GA: G3 Ministries, 2023. https://hymnary.org/hymn/PHLG2023/315.

Renovaré Institute. "About the Renovaré Institute." Renovaré. https://renovare.org/institute/overview.

Robert, Henry M. *Robert's Rules of Order*. Chicago: S. C. Griggs, 1876.

Robinson, Martin. *Rediscovering the Celts: The True Witness from Western Shores*. London: SPCK, 2000.

Rognlien, Bob. *Experiential Worship: Encountering God with Heart, Soul, Mind, and Strength*. Colorado Springs, CO: NavPress, 2005.

Root, Andrew. *The Pastor in a Secular Age: Ministry to People Who No Longer Need a God*. Grand Rapids: Baker Academic, 2019.

Root, Andrew, and Blair D. Bertrand. *When Church Stops Working: A Future for Your Congregation Beyond More Money, Programs, and Innovation*. Grand Rapids: Baker, 2023.

Roxburgh, Alan J. *Joining God in the Great Unraveling: Where We Are and What I've Learned*. Eugene, OR: Wipf & Stock, 2021.

———. *Joining God, Remaking Church, Changing the World: The New Shape of the Church in Our Time*. New York: Morehouse, 2015.

Roxburgh, Alan J., and Martin Robinson. *Practices for the Refounding of God's People: The Missional Challenge of the West*. New York: Church Publishing, 2018.

The Salvation Army. "About Us." The Salvation Army Southern Nevada. https://www.salvationarmysouthernnevada.org/about-the-salvation-army.

Sayers, Mark. *Disappearing Church: From Cultural Relevance to Gospel Resilience*. Chicago: Moody, 2016.

Shadowlight, Simon. "Do You Have the Courage to Live Prophetic Spirituality?" Mile Hi Church, Mar. 1, 2021. https://www.milehichurch.org/courage-to-live-prophetic-spirituality/.

Shakespeare, William. *Hamlet*. Edited by Barbara Mowat et al. Folger Shakespeare Library (website). Washington, DC: Folger Shakespeare Library. https://www.folger.edu/explore/shakespeares-works/hamlet/read/1/5/.

Simpson, Ray. *Celtic Worship Through the Year*. Abingdon: Bible Reading Fellowship, 2008.

———. *Exploring Celtic Spirituality: Historic Roots for Our Future*. London: Hodder & Stoughton, 1995.

———. "Introducing the International Community of Aidan and Hilda." Ray Simpson: Contemporary Celtic Christianity. https://www.raysimpson.org/introducing-the-international-community-aidan-and-hilda.

Bibliography

Smiech, Andrzej. "Conversations That Matter: Post-Covid-19 Changeover in Leadership Interactions." *Forbes*, Oct. 20, 2021. https://www.forbes.com/councils/forbescoachescouncil/2021/10/20/conversations-that-matter-post-covid-19-changeover-in-leadership-interactions/.

Snyder, Howard A. *The Community of the King*. Downers Grove, IL: InterVarsity, 2010.

Stott, John R. W. *The Cross of Christ*. Downers Grove, IL: InterVarsity, 1986.

Suzuki, Shinichi. *Nurtured by Love: The Classic Approach to Talent Education*. Translated by Waltraud Suzuki. Tokyo: Suzuki, 1983.

Sweet, Leonard. *From Tablet to Table: Where Community Is Found and Identity Is Formed*. Colorado Springs, CO: NavPress, 2014.

———. *Soul Tsunami: Sink or Swim in New Millennium Culture*. Grand Rapids: Zondervan, 1999.

Sweet, Leonard, and Mark Chironna. *Rings of Fire: Walking in Faith Through a Volcanic Future*. Colorado Springs, CO: NavPress, 2019.

Swoboda, A. J. *Subversive Sabbath: The Surprising Power of Rest in a Nonstop World*. Grand Rapids: Brazos, 2018.

Thurman, Howard. *The Negro Spiritual Speaks of Life and Death*. Richmond, IN: Friends United, 1975.

Toffler, Alvin. *Future Shock*. New York: Bantam, 2022.

Tozer, A. W. *The Pursuit of God*. Saffron Walden, UK: Christian Publications, 1968.

———. "Worship: The Missing Jewel." In *Whatever Happened to Worship?*, edited by Gerald B. Smith, 96. Camp Hill, PA: WingSpread, 2012.

Twells, Henry. "At Even, Ere the Sun Was Set." In *Ancient and Modern: Hymns and Songs for Refreshing Worship*, #13. London: Hymns Ancient & Modern, 2013. https://hymnary.org/text/at_even_ere_the_sun_was_set.

Warren, Rick. "Why You Need a Church Family with Rick Warren." Oct. 15, 2018. Video, 36:51. https://www.youtube.com/watch?v=W89x9JfULMc.

Wikipedia. "Camino de Santiago," Wikimedia Foundation. Last modified Feb. 5, 2025. https://en.wikipedia.org/wiki/Camino_de_Santiago.

———. "Moral Character." Wikimedia Foundation. Last modified Nov. 2, 2024. https://en.wikipedia.org/wiki/Moral_character.

———. "Taizé Community." Wikimedia Foundation. Last modified Jan. 12, 2025. https://en.wikipedia.org/wiki/Taiz%C3%A9_Community.

Willard, Dallas. *The Allure of Gentleness: Defending the Faith in the Manner of Jesus*. New York: HarperOne, 2015. Kindle.

———. *The Divine Conspiracy: Rediscovering our Hidden Life in God*. New York: HarperOne, 1998.

———. *Renovation of the Heart: Putting on the Character of Christ*. Colorado Springs, CO: NavPress, 2002.

Woodley, Randy S., et al. *Decolonizing Evangelicalism: An 11:59 p.m. Conversation*. Eugene, OR: Cascade, 2020.

Wright, N. T. *After You Believe: Why Christian Character Matters*. New York: HarperOne, 2010.

———. *Surprised by Hope: Rethinking Heaven, the Resurrection, and the Mission of the Church*. New York: HarperOne, 2008.

Zimmer, Sandra. "Famous vs Great." Sandra Zimmer and the Self-Expression Center. https://www.sandrazimmer.com/blog/famous-vs-great/.

www.ingramcontent.com/pod-product-compliance
Lightning Source LLC
Chambersburg PA
CBHW051106160426
43193CB00010B/1341